STAR TREK
Collectibles

Classic Serie ☆ Next Generation ☆ Deep Space Nine ☆ Voyager

Ursula Augustin

Schiffer Publishing Ltd

4880 Lower Valley Rd. Atglen, PA 19310 USA

Translated by Dr. Edward Force,
Central Connecticut State University.

Digital Photography by Martina Mayr and Peter Viechtbauer, Repro
Mayr, Donauwörth; Elmar Ruischmann.

Additional photo material was made available by Thomas Brückl, Silvia
Felser, Marc Tacke, and Robert Amper.

Copyright © 1997 by Schiffer Publishing Ltd.
Library of Congress Catalog Card Number: 97-80095

ISBN: 0-7643-0378-3
Printed in the United States of America

Published by Schiffer Publishing Ltd.
4880 Lower Valley Road
Atglen, PA 19310
Phone: (610) 593-1777; Fax: (610) 593-2002
Please write for a free catalog.
This book may be purchased from the publisher.
Please include $3.95 for shipping.

Try your bookstore first.

We are interested in hearing from authors
with book ideas on related subjects.

Table of Contents

Dedication

For my friend Doris,
You're always there when I need you! Your patience is as endless as the galaxies. Without you, this book would never have come into being!

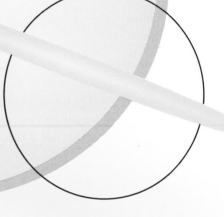

Acknowledgements

I offer very hearty thanks to:

Dirk Bartholomä,
who turned this project over to me.

Elmar Rutschmann,
who was always at my side during its writing, and who cuts a great figure in uniform.

Andreas Kliem
who made the materials for most of the illustrations available.

Tom Haver,
for lending me his really precious Playmates.

Ralf Breiden,
for specialized advice and support.

Lothar and Reiner,
You already know for what!

Sylvia Strybuc
for very special insights into fandom.

Captain Cozy — U.S.S. Sonderpreis
"Rock till you drop!"

Robert Amper
and all the other crew members of the U.S.S. Highlander
for the unbelievable adventures of our play crew!

and finally, to all those who helped on this project and, for lack of space, cannot be mentioned by name!

There's a Light in the Darkness of everybody's life!

Star Trek Collectibles — or Why the Starship Enterprise?

How could we, the children of the 1960s, who saw the first appearance of the Starship Enterprise on German television in the autumn of 1972 (usually on black-and-white screens, holding out against our parents' protests and the sports simultaneously broadcast on another channel!)—we who followed the adventures of Captain James T. Kirk, his First Officer Spock (what I wouldn't have given then for those ears!), "Bonesl" McCoy, the good-natured Chief Handyman Scotty, the superhumanly beautiful Uhura with the "button in her ear," and all the rest of the crew—how could we even begin to suspect how much *Star Trek* would influence and even change all our lives in the next 25 years! If we had, those who are still fans of *Star Trek* today would surely have preserved everything that was published on this subject, thus creating a solid and, above all, valuable basis for a collection.

Unfortunately, few of us thought of it then, and so a lot of material was lost, never to be recovered (photo novels from the program publication *Gong* or old "Bravo" posters, for example). Collectors would pay a small fortune for the originals today, or at least console themselves with color copies. And when one thinks of the first moveable play figures of Kirk, Spock, and company, barely 15 centimeters tall, that were thrown off somewhere sometime after a wild game ... the grownup collector still gets tears in his eyes remembering that he once owned them and can only get them back today at a film collectors' fair or a dealer's table at a convention for a lot of hard-earned money.

This book has arisen out of those nostalgic feelings. I am one of those children from the time before cable television, remote controls, and videotaping, who took, once a week, those "first steps into space" with Kirk, Spock, and company and instantly felt at home on the U.S.S. Enterprise — NC 1701 — exploring strange worlds "where no man has gone before." Ever since Neil Armstrong's first steps on the moon in 1969 — which I was allowed to watch live in the middle of the night at the age of six — we have all dreamed of a better world, of overcoming boundaries and traveling to distant galaxies. We acted it all out in our own way in the woods near home, with phasers we carved ourselves out of wood, wearing blue, red, or yellow pullovers lovingly decorated with emblems and stripes by Grandma and carrying cassette recorders that were transformed in our into tricorders in our imaginations, long before corresponding toys could be bought here.

Today — barely 25 years later — I would give a small fortune for the wooden phaser and my beautiful blue pullover, but both have disappeared into a nexus (a hole in time), and so I have limited myself to flying through space in my imagination now and then with my friends from the "Highlander" role-playing project, and showing and documenting things here in this book that can still be had, and that can give a Star Trek collector a little joy.

Augsburg, March 1997
Ursula Augustin

P.S.:
With the immense quantities of Star Trek merchandise available all over the world, we can only portray a very small sampling of them because this book had to be finished within strict time constraints. My teacher and I brought all the material we could gather during the three months of pre-production into the photo studio and photographed them. I hope the results are pleasing.

I ask that you send any encouragement, suggestions for improvement, criticism, or other correspondence directly to the publisher (Schiffer Books Ltd., 4880 Lower Valley Road, Atglen, PA 19310).

I will read all correspondence and consider your suggestions and wishes — as far as possible — in further editions! Whoever can loan us material for photographing or would like to appear in the Forum pages should likewise get in touch with the publisher, I promise to respond, sooner or later.

Explanation of Abbreviations

In the Star Trek universe we differentiate among different series:

We begin with the original television series of the 1960s, today usually called **TOS** (The Original Series), or simply **Classic**.

Next come the cinema films — and here things get more difficult. I have decided to call them **The Movies** — usually citing the film number (for example, *Star Trek: First Contact* thus becomes Movie VIII).

Then come seven years of *Star Trek: The Next Generation*. Abbreviated, it is called simply **TNG**.

It is the same for *Star Trek: Deep Space 9*: **DS9**.

And this is also true of the newest child in the Trek universe: **VOY** means nothing else but the Starship "Voyager."

All other pertinent information should be spelled out in the photo captions, with the exception of often-cited manufacturers, who are usually mentioned just once if their products dominate an entire page. The listed prices are averaged calculations from the catalogs of five Star Trek dealers we consulted in Germany, and should serve only as guidelines.

Figures

Star Trek action figures enjoy universal popularity among fans — both the small plastic figures and the larger collectors' figures, which are some 30 centimeters tall and complete with detailed cloth clothing.

About the small Playmates, it should be noted that they are always worth considerably more when packed in the original blister cards than when they have been unpacked and used. This is because (and this is especially true of the more valuable figures) the package contributes to the value. Remember, it is relatively easy for a capable painter or modelmaker to use paint and a steady hand to turn a mass-produced figure, such as the Data of the first series who wore a yellow uniform, into a much more valuable piece (such as a later Data figure that wore a different color uniform). So who would want to buy an unpacked figure?

The varying values within a series are also of interest — some of the figures appeared in the United States with a trading card, others with a POG. The figures that came with a POG are usually somewhat more valuable than those with a trading card. Why is that? Well, there were fewer packages with the POG, and thus the value changed.

The figures of the first series, which came on the market in Germany in 1992, were not packed on blistercards like the American ones, but in boxes. That makes these figures, which one can still pick up at rather low prices in Germany today, interesting to the American collector. They sell for up to $25 in the United States. The "Borg" and "Gowron" figures are also of interest. When one unpacks these figures, one finds that the "accessories" (weapons, parts, etc.) for the German figures are made of a very soft plastic material, unlike the hard plastic parts with the American versions.

The values in our figure chapter can only serve as "guidelines," since price variations among the action figures are enormous. If you're lucky, and have a good dealer, you'll pay an acceptable price, though you can also pay a high price for a rare figure. So if you can find a figure in its original packing for a lower price than we've listed, you can buy it with confidence — it's probably a real bargain!

1. Classic Set

Lt. Hikaru Sulu
Lt. Nyota Uhura
Cmdr. Spock
Capt. James T. Kirk
Dr. Leonard McCoy
Engineer Montgomery Scott
Ensign Pavel Chekov
together as a set
package becomes Classic bridge
$115

2. Command Set

Cmdr. Benjamin Sisko
Major Kira Nerys
Major James T. Kirk in dress uniform
Cmdr. Spock in dress uniform
Capt. Jean-Luc Picard in dress uniform
together as a set
package shows space
in the background
$80

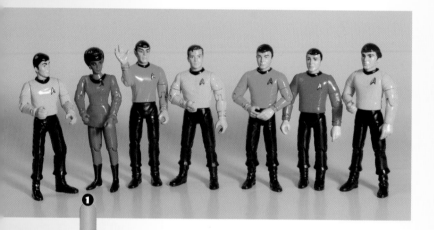

3. Lt. Cmdr. Montgomery Scott

4. Lt. Hikaru Sulu

From the pilot sequel *Where No Man Has Gone Before*, sold together in a set at the Alabama Convention in 1996, limited edition of 10,000 figures
$310

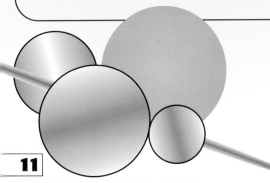

FIGUREN

1. Cmdr. Kruge
Classic "Movie Series"
$15

General Chang
Classic "Movie Series"
$15

3. Admiral James T. Kirk
Classic "Movie Series"
$15

4. Lt. Hikaru Sulu
Classic "Movie Series"
$12

5. Khan Noonian Singh
Classic "Movie Series"
$20

Lt. Nyota Uhura
$20

Dr. Leonard H. McCoy
$20

6. Ensign Saavik
Classic "Movie Series"
$15

Cmdr. Spock
$15

Martia
$30

If one collects all five figures from the motion picture series, one can assemble a "V'ger-Scene." Each package contains a piece of the scene.

7. B'Ethor
$35

8. Lursa
$15

The Klingon sisters from the house of Duras (*Generation* series, 1994)

9. Capt. Katheryn Janeway
$12

10. Cmdr. Chakotay
$12

11. Ensign Harry Kim
with or without phaser: $25

12. Lt. Tom Paris
$12

13. Neelix
$12

14. The Holodoctor
(holographic medical emergency program with unknown chances of development) $15

15. Lt. B'Elanna Torres
$12

Voyager, erste Serie, 1996

FIGUREN

1. Cmdr. William T. Riker
ST: TNG, 1st series, 1992 $20

2. Lt. Cmdr. Data
ST: TNG, 1st series, 1992 $20

3. Dr. Beverly Crusher
ST: TNG, 2nd series, 1993
with trading card: $25
ST: TNG, 3rd series, 1994
with POG: $30

4. Capt. Jean-Luc Picard
ST: TNG, 1st series, 1992 $20

5. Counselor Deanna Troi
ST: TNG, 7th season series, 1994 $28

6. Lt. Cmdr. Geordie LaForge
ST: TNG, 1st series, 1992: $20
with removable visor: $38

7. Lt. Worf
ST: TNG, 1st series, 1992 $20

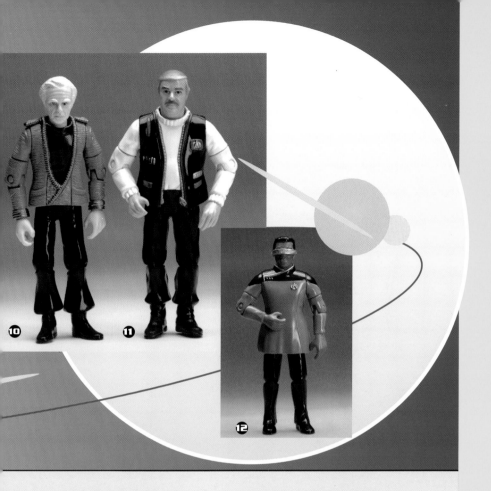

. Data in Forties Outfit
T: TNG, Holodeck Series, 1995 $20

. Jean-Luc Picard as Dixon Hill
T: TNG, 7th season series, 1994 $20

0. Admiral Leonard H. McCoy
T: TNG, 2nd series, 1993 $20

11. Capt. Montgomery Scott
ST: TNG, 2nd series, 1993 $20

12. Lt. Cmdr. Geordie LaForge in dress uniform
ST: TNG, 2nd series, 1993
with trading card: $20
ST: TNG, 3rd series, 1994
with POG: $25

FIGUREN

1. Q in DS9 uniform
ST: DS9, 2nd series, 1995 $20

2. Q in Judge's Robe
(also known as "intergalactic annoyance")
ST: TNG, 7th season series, 1994 $25

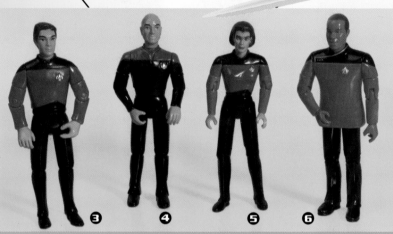

3. Ensign Wesley Crusher
ST: TNG, 2nd series, 1993 $20

4. Capt. Jean-Luc Picard in DS9 uniform
ST: DS9, 2nd series, 1995 $20

5. Ensign Ro Laren
ST: TNG, 1995 $30

6. Cmdr. Benjamin Sisko
dress uniform; ST: DS9, 2nd series, '95 $15

7. Mordock the Benzite
ST: TNG, 2nd series, 1993
with trading card: $20
ST: TNG, 3rd series, 1994
with POG: $30

8. Cadet Wesley Crusher
ST: TNG, 2nd series, 1993
with trading card: $20
ST: TNG, 3rd series, 1994
with POG: $30

9. Guinan
ST: TNG, 2nd series, 1993
with trading card: $28
ST" TNG, 3rd series, 1994
with POG: $30

10. Q in TNG uniform
ST: TNG, 2nd series, 1993
with trading card: $20
ST: TNG, 3rd series, 1994
with POG: $25

1

2

1. Lt. Cmdr. Data

ST: TNG, 7th season series, 1994
from the episode "Redemption"
limited, $400

2. Lt. Tasha Yar

ST: TNG, 1995 $20

3. Counselor Deanna Troi

ST: TNG, 2nd series, 1993
with trading card: $12
ST: TNG, 3rd series, 1994
with POG: $25

4 Worf in Klingon outfit

(chrome-plated version)
ST: TNG, holodeck series, 1995 $15

5. Gowron

ST: TNG, 1st series, 1992
Standard version: $20
without gold details: $38

6. Romulan

ST: TNG, 1st series, 1992 $20

7. Commander Sela

ST: TNG, 2nd series, 1993
with trading card: $20
ST: TNG, 3rd series, 1994
with POG: $25

FIGUREN

⚠ WARNING:
CHOKING HAZARD - Small parts.
Not for children under 3 years.

Ages 4 and up.

STAR TREK ™

AS SEEN IN THE EPISODE "TAPESTRY"!

CAPTAIN
JEAN LUC PICARD®

FROM THE HIT T.V. SHOW
STAR TREK
THE NEXT GENERATION®

TAPESTRY
ACCESSORIES:
DOM-JOT ROD
CHESS SET
DUFFEL BAG
DRINKING MUG

BONUS:
STARFLEET
ACTION BASE

NEW
ONLY 1701 RELEASED!
LIMITED
EDITION

Asst. No. 6430
Stock No. 6442

Playmates®

❶

1. Ensign Jean-Luc Picard
ST: TNG, 1995
from the episode "Tapestry"
limited to 1701 pieces
$1,100

2. Capt. Jean-Luc Picard
ST: TNG, 3rd series, 1994
$25

3. Locutus of Borg
ST: TNG, 2nd series, 1993
with trading card: $28
ST: TNG, 3rd series, 1994
with POG: $37

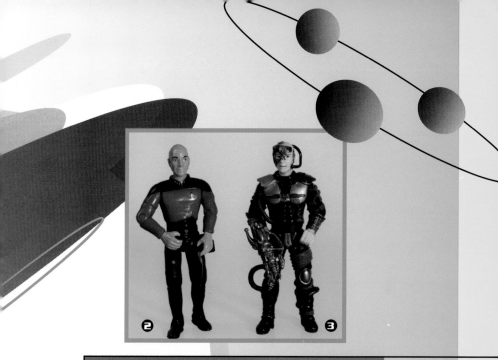

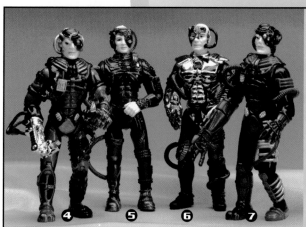

4. Borg
with chromed arm part
ST: TNG, 2nd series, 1993
with trading card: $12
ST: TNG, 3rd series, 1994
with POG: $25

5. Hugh Borg
(third of five)
ST: TNG, 7th season series, 1994 $25

6. Locutus of Borg
(chrome-plated version)
ST: TNG, holodeck series, 1995 $28

7. Borg
ST: TNG, 1st series, 1992
normal value: $20
with mirror-image photo on
back of package: $38

FIGUREN

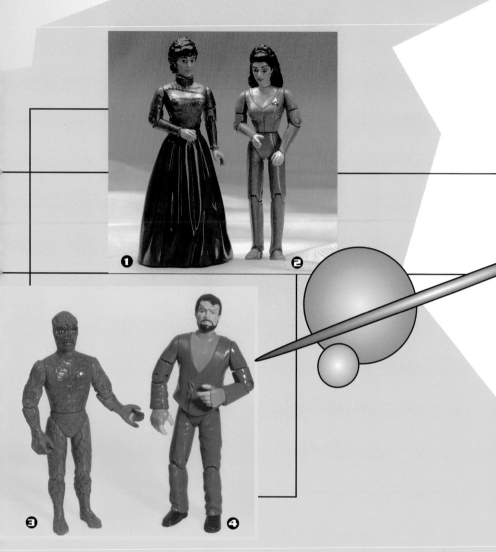

1. Lwaxana Troi
ST: TNG, 1995 $15

2. Counselor Deanna Troi
ST: TNG, 1st series, 1992 $15

3. Lt. Geordie LaForge as Tarchanian alien
ST: TNG, 7th season series, 1994 $15

4. William T. Riker as Malcorian
ST: TNG, 7th season series, 1994 $15

5. Lt. Thomas Riker

ST: TNG. 7th season series, 1994
limited edition $280

6. Lt. Thomas Riker
in original package

This figure is identical to that of William T. Riker (Page
14, No. 1), the only difference being in coloring —
Thomas wears the yellow uniform of the technicians.
For that reason, this figure is this valuable only in the
original package, as a capable hobbyist could repaint an
unpacked figure.

FIGUREN

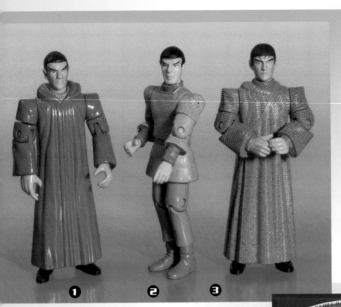

1. Jean-Luc Picard as Romulan
ST: TNG, 7th season series, 1994 $15

2. Ambassador Spock
ST: TNG, 2nd series, 1993,
with trading card: $20
ST: TNG, 3rd series, 1994,
with POG: $25

3. Data as Romulan
ST: TNG, 7th season series, 1994 $15

4. Ambassador Spock
in original package with trading card

5. Dathon, the Tamarian
ST: 2nd series, 1993
with trading card: $20
ST: TNG, 3rd series, 1994
with POG: $55

6. Ferengi
ST: TNG, 1st series, 1992
standard version: $20
without black color on
legs and boots: $38

7. Vorgon
ST: TNG, 1st series, 1992
with trading card: $20
ST: 3rd series, 1994
with POG: $55

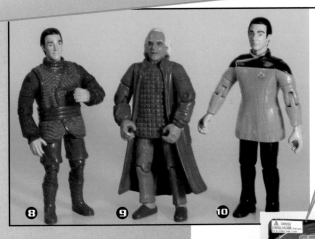

8. Lore
ST: TNG, 2nd series, 1993
with trading card: $20
ST: TNG, 3rd series, 1994
with POG: $20

9. Dr. Noonian Soong
ST: TNG, 7th season series, 1994
$15

10. Lt. Cmdr. Data in dress uniform
ST: TNG, 7th season series, 1994
$20

11. Dr. Noonian Soong
in original package on blister card

FIGUREN

1. Gowron as Klingon Chief
ST: TNG, 7th season series, 1994 $50

2. Esoqq, the Chalna
ST: TNG, 7th season series, 1994 $95

⊟

3. Lt. Tasha Yar
ST: TNG, 1995
from the episode "Yesterday's Enterprise"
limited to 1701 pieces.
$750

FIGUREN

1. Lt. Reginald Barclay
ST: TNG, 7th season series, 1994 $20

2. Chief Miles O'Brien
ST: TNG, 2nd series, 1995 $20

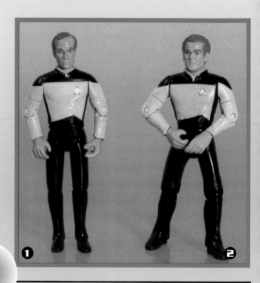

3. Worf in rescue outfit
ST: TNG, 7th season series, 1994 $20

4. K'Ehleyr
ST: TNG, 2nd series, 1993
with trading card: $20
ST: TNG, 3rd series, 1994
with POG: $25

5. Lt. Cmdr. Data in DS9 uniform
ST: TNG, 1995 $15

6. Data in 40s outfit
ST: TNG Holodeck series, 1995 $20

7. Nausicaan
ST: TNG, 1995 $20

FIGUREN

1. Cmdr. Benjamin Sisko
(Mail-order Sisko)
Could only be ordered along with a video game in the United States, thus only as a limited special issue without accessories.
$95

2. Lt. Jadzia Dax
ST: DS9, 1st series, 1994 $30

3. Chief Miles O'Brien
ST: DS9, 1st series, 1994 $25

4. Jake Sisko
ST: DS9, 2nd series, 1995 $12

5. Dr. Julian Bashir
ST: DS9, 2nd series, 1995 $20

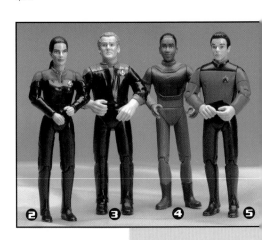

6. Admiral William T. Riker

ST: TNG, 1995
from the episode "All Good Things"
$12

7. Jean-Luc Picard

ST: TNG, 1995
from the episode "All Good Things"
$12

FIGUREN

1. Grand Nagus Zek

ST: DS9, 1995
$15

2. Elim Garak

ST: DS9, 1995
$12

3. Rom and Nog
ST: DS9, 2nd series, 1995
together $20

4. Morn
ST: DS9, 1st series, 1994 $25

5. Quark
ST: DS9, 1st series, 1994 $25

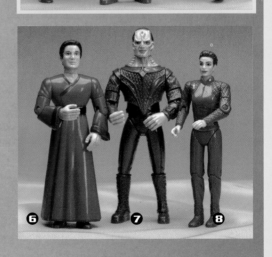

6. Vedek Bareil
ST: DS9, 2nd series, 1995 $20

7. Gul Dukat
ST: DS9, 1st series, 1994 $30

8. Major Kira Nerys
ST: DS9, 1st series, 1994 $25

FIGUREN

1. Lt. Thomas Riker
ST: DS9, 2nd series, 1995
$20

2. Tosk
ST: DS9, 2nd series, 1995
$12

3. Worf in DS9 uniform
ST: DS9, 1995: $12

4. Cadet Worf
ST: Starfleet Academy, 1996
with "Starfleet Academy" CD-Rom $20

5. Cadet Geordie LaForge
ST: Starfleet Academy, 1996
with "Starfleet Academy" CD-Rom $20

6. Cadet William T. Riker
ST: Starfleet Academy, 1996
with "Starfleet Academy" CD-Rom $20

7. Cadet Jean-Luc Picard
ST: Starfleet Academy, 1996
with "Starfleet Academy" CD-Rom $20

FIGUREN

1. Borg

Alien Edition, 2nd series, 1995
$38

2. Worf

Alien Edition, 2nd series, 1995
$38

3. Capt. Jean-Luc Picard

Command Edition, 1994
$30

4. Guinan

Federation Edition, 1995
$30

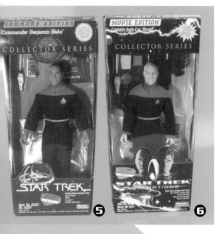

5. Cmdr. Benjamin Sisko

Command Edition, 1994
$30

6. Capt. Jean-Luc Picard

Movie Edition, 1994
$30

7. Lt. Cmdr. Geordie LaForge

Movie Edition, 1994
$30

8. Lt. Cmdr. Data

Movie Edition, 1994
$30

9. Dr. Leonard H. McCoy

Federation Edition, 1995
$38

10. Lt. Cmdr. Montgomery Scott

Federation Edition, 1996
$38

FIGUREN

1. Dr. Beverly Crusher
Starfleet Edition, 1995
$38

2. Cmdr. Deanna Troi
Starfleet Edition, 1995
$38

3. Capt. Jean-Luc Picard
in dress uniform
Starfleet Edition, 1995
$30

4. Capt. James T. Kirk
in dress uniform
Starfleet Edition, 1995
$38

5. Lt. Cmdr. Geordie LaForge
Starfleet Edition, 1995
$30

6. Cmdr. William T. Riker
Starfleet Edition, 1995
$30

7. Lt. Cmdr. Data
Starfleet Edition, 1995
$30

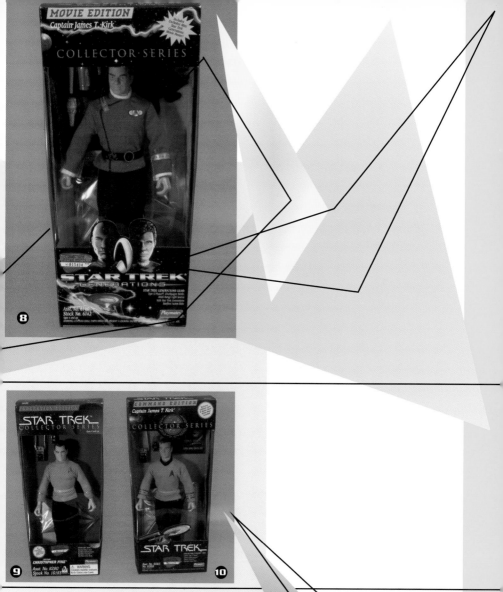

8. Capt. James T. Kirk
Movie Edition, 1994
$90

9. Capt. James T. Kirk
Command Edition, 1994
$75

10. Capt. Christopher Pike
Command Edition, 1996
$30

FIGUREN

1. Cmdr. Spock
Exclusive Figure Target Market $65

2. Lt. Hikaru Sulu
Exclusive Figure Target Market $65

3. Lt. Cmdr. M. Scott
Exclusive Figure Target Market $65

Figures 1 to 3 wear the first uniforms from the pilot, *Where No Man Has Gone Before*

4. Cmdr. William T. Riker
First Contact Edition 1996 $50

5. Capt. Jean-Luc Picard
First Contact Edition, 1996 $50

6. Lt. Cmdr. Data
First Contact Edition 1996 $38

7. Capt. Jean-Luc Picard
First Contact Edition, 1996 $50

8. Zephram Cochrane
First Contact Edition, 1996 $50

9. Capt. Jean-Luc Picard
ST: First Contact Edition, 1996
$12

10. Borg
ST: First Contact Edition, 1996
$12

11. Cmdr. Deanna Troi
ST: First Contact Edition, 1996
$12

12. Dr. Beverly Crusher
ST: First Contact Edition, 1996
$12

13. Lt. Cmdr. Worf
ST: First Contact Edition, 1996
$12

14. Cmdr. William T. Riker
ST: First Contact Edition, 1996
$12

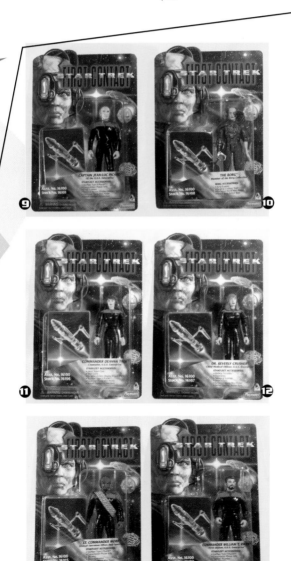

FIGUREN

1. Bridge Playset

Playmates-Bandai, 1993, without figures
$150

2 Bridge Playset

plus the following figures, back to front:

Lt. Worf

ST: TNG, 2nd series, 1993
with trading card: $12
ST: TNG, 3rd series, 1994
with POG: $25

Lt. Tasha Yar

ST: TNG, 1995
$18

Cmdr. William T. Riker

ST: TNG, 2nd series, 1993
with trading card: $12
ST: TNG, 3rd series, 1994
with POG: $25

Capt. Jean-Luc Picard

ST: TNG, 2nd series, 1993
with trading card: $12
ST: TNG, 3rd series, 1994
with POG: $25

Counselor Deanna Troi

ST: TNG, first series, 1992: $12

Lt. Cmdr. Data

ST: TNG, 2nd series, 1993
with trading card: $12
ST: TNG, 3rd series, 1994
with POG: $25

Lt. Geordie LaForge

ST: TNG, 2nd series, 1993: $12

3. Cmdr. William T. Riker

Tin figure
Rawcliffe, USA, 1993
hand-painted
Augsburg, Germany
$30

4. Capt. Jean-Luc Picard

Tin figure
Rawcliffe, USA, 1993
hand-painted
Augsburg, Germany
$30

5. Cmdr. Spock

Tin figure
Rawcliffe, USA, 1993
hand-painted
Augsburg, Germany
$30

6. Capt. James T. Kirk

Tin figure
Rawcliffe, USA, 1993
hand-painted
Augsburg, Germany
$30

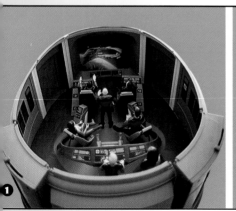

7. Capt. James T. Kirk
MEGO, USA, 1974
sold for $6 new
present value $65

8. Klingon
MEGO, USA, 1974
Sold new for $6
present value $75

9. Sulu
miniature
Applause, USA, 1986
limited edition, 6,000
pieces
$38

FIGUREN

Barbie & Ken

STAR TREK GIFTSET

1. Star Trek Barbie & Ken in Classic Uniforms

Mattel, USA, 1996
limited edition
from $110

2. Mr. Spock

V.I.B's: Very Important Bears
Bear Trek — live long and prosbear!
North American Bear Inc., USA, 1990
sale price $155

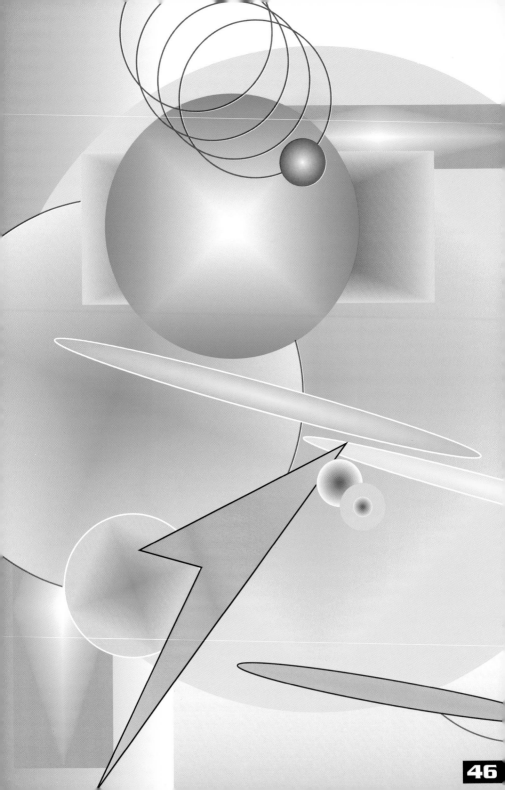

Uniforms

There's no other similar large group of fans in the world (with the exception of *Rocky Horror Picture Show* fans — but that is a different universe, and a very different "cult") that dons costumes as happily and as well as those within the *Star Trek* orbit.

Armin Shimerman (Quark) put it well while speaking with a guest panel before a room of some 2,500 people (some 1,800 of them properly uniformed!): "In America, one sees at most a quarter of the fans at conventions costumed, in Germany three-quarters. It looks like the Paramount canteen during a lunch break!"

In costume and look-alike competitions at conventions, one can admire many often-beautifully costumed people who exhibit every possible kind of attire, uniform, equipment, etc. In this chapter we show mainly the uniforms from the various series and movies — everything from ready-made clothing to those costumes partly made with the help of professionals, and those made completely by commercial tailors.

In the Forum (starting on Page 192) are some active fans who make everything themselves.

Often it is just a question of money for the "adorer" as to whether he or she will pay some $55 for a ready-made uniform top or have a perfect uniform made at a much higher price.

In any case, anything is possible.

1. Classic Minidress

in blue (science and medicine), self-made by Susanne Menzel. The material cost about $125

2. Classic Uniform Dress "Uhura"

Rubie's, USA, 1990 $45

1

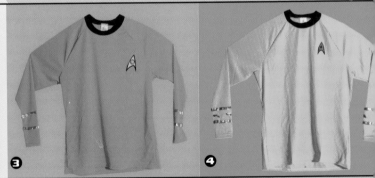

3

4

3. Classic Uniform Shirt "Spock"

Rubie's, USA, 1990
$40

4. Classic Uniform Shirt "Kirk"

Rubie's, USA, 1990
$40

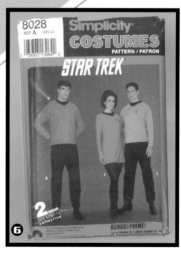

5. Classic Uniform Shirt "Scotty"

Rubie's, USA, 1990
$40

6. Classic Costume Patterns

Patterns for minidress, shirt, and trousers
with iron-on insignia. Simplicity Pattern
Company Inc., USA, 1992
$18

Uniform/Kleidung

1. "Star Trek Card Game" T-shirt

American Flag, USA
$18
(advertising for the German card game)

2. "Jim, it's inhuman" Classic T-shirt

Network Company, Ltd., GB, 1996
$25

3. Baseball Cap, Classic Command Emblem

embroidered cotton
GEM Inc., USA, 1995
$20
(worn privately by actor George Takei)

4. Movie Uniform

with all insignia; ready-made
single piece
Robert Amper

5. Movie Uniform

$220 tailor-made
$95 for fabric and lining
$110 for metal insignia

STAR TREK.
MOVIES
UNIFORM PATTERNS

Women's
Jacket
#0801

6. Pattern for women's jacket

Lady's jacket
(men's also available)
R.P.C., USA, 1987
$20

Uniform/Kleidung

1. TNG Jumpsuit deluxe

Lady's overall with rank pins and plastic communicator
Rubie's, USA
$75

2. TNG Uniform Shirt

with rank pins and metal communicator
Filmwelt, Berlin, 1995
$55

TNG Uniform Trousers

Filmwelt, Berlin, 1995
$55

3. TNG Uniform Pattern: Women's Jacket

P.P.C., USA, 1987
$12

4. TNG Admiral's Jacket

Single piece
Chris Augustin
$220 tailor-made
$95 for fabric,
$65 for insignia

5. TNG Duty Uniform Jacket

of deerskin
with undershirt
tailored by Susanne Menzel
$220 for material

STAR TREK THE NEXT GENERATION
Women's Jacket $7.95 #0810
UNIFORM PATTERNS

❸

1

2

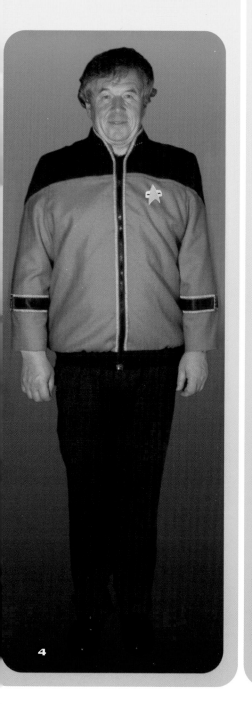

4

5

1. TNG Borg T-shirt

"Resistance is futile"
printed front and back
P.P.C., USA
$28

2. TNG Borg T-shirt

"Your culture will be assimilated"
printed front and back
P.P.C., USA
$28

3. TNG Borg T-shirt

"Hugh — Third of Five"
printed front and back
P.P.C., USA
$28

4. TNG T-shirt

"Patrick Stewart as Jean-Luc Picard"
printed front and back
P.P.C., USA
$30

5. TNG T-shirt

"Brent Spiner as Data"
P.P.C., USA
$30

Uniform/Kleidung

3. DS9
Bajoran Uniform

Rubie's, USA, 1994
$75

4. DS9
Bajoran Uniform

tailored by Susanne Menzel
cotton; sleeves of deerskin
$155 for material

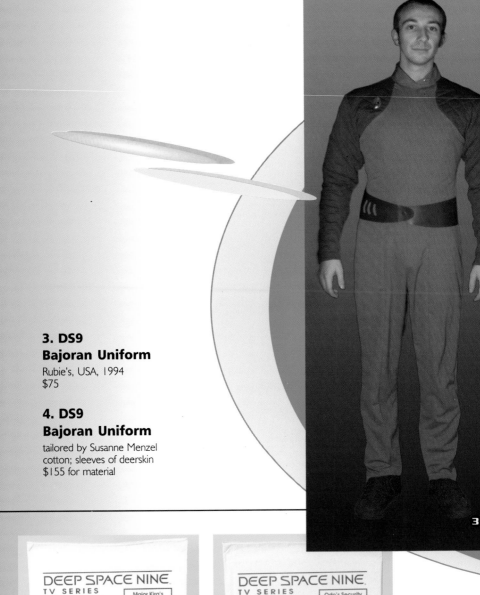

3

DEEP SPACE NINE.
TV SERIES
UNIFORM
PATTERNS

Major Kira's
Uniform Jacket
$11.95 #0817

❶

DEEP SPACE NINE.
TV SERIES
UNIFORM
PATTERNS

Odo's Security
Uniform
$11.95 #0816

❷

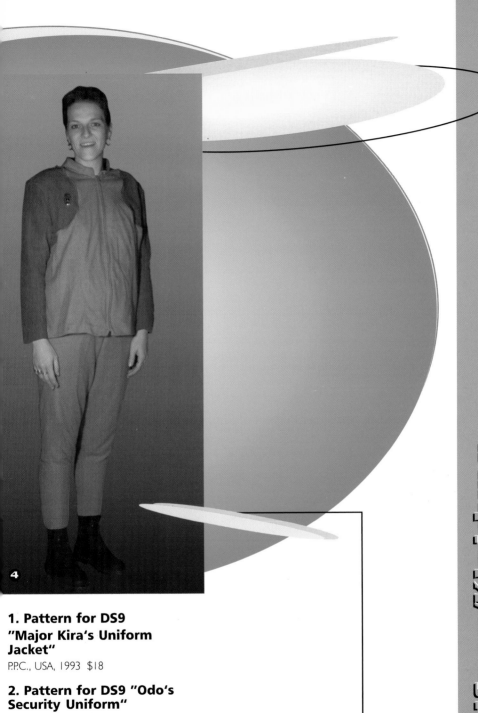

4

1. Pattern for DS9 "Major Kira's Uniform Jacket"

P.P.C., USA, 1993 $18

2. Pattern for DS9 "Odo's Security Uniform"

P.P.C., USA, 1993 $18

Uniform/Kleidung

1. DS9/VOY Jumpsuit deluxe — Command

Lady's overall with undershirt
Rubie's, USA, 1996
$75

2. DS9/VOY Uniform deluxe — Engineering/Security

Uniform jacket with undershirt
Rubie's, USA
$55

ght:

TNG Dress Uniform

gle piece, tailored by Robert Amper
20 tailor-made
5 for fabric and lining
5 for insignia

enter:
me as Page 52, Picture 2

ft:
me as Page 58, Picture 1

*he Starfleet Academy Class of '96 greets
e rest of the universe!*

1. DS9/VOY Uniform Shirt deluxe — Medical/Science

with undershirt
Rubie's, USA
$55

2. DS9/VOY Jumpsuit deluxe — Command

with undershirt
Rubie's, USA
$75

3. VOY T-shirt with Voyager logo

American Flag, USA
$18

④

4. Traveling Bag

with embroidered "Voyager"
Creation Convention, USA, 1996
$38
(That Captain Janeway always has
everything at hand, even on
away missions...)

5. Voyager Baseball Cap

Gold-embroidered lettering, cotton
P.P.C., USA
$20

1. Ferengi Make-up Kit

Rubie's, USA, 1994
$25

2. First Contact T-shirt

Picture of Jean-Luc Picard
"The Line Must Be Drawn Here"
Gildan, 1996
$25

3. First Contact T-shirt

Gildan, 1996
$25

4. First Contact T-shirt

Promotional T-shirt for film premiere
P.P.C., USA, 1996
$30

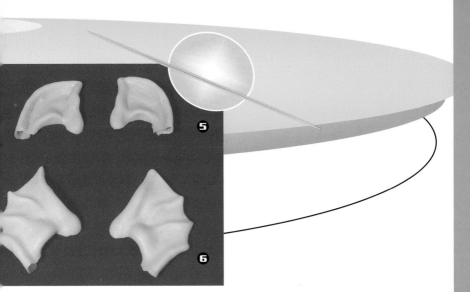

5. Vulcan Ears

Made of latex, attached with liquid latex
Augsburg, Germany
$12

6. Alien Ears

Made of latex, attached with liquid latex
Augsburg, Germany
$15

7. Small Bajoran Nose

Made of latex foam, Scarecrow, USA
$10

8. Large Bajoran Nose

Made of latex foam, Scarecrow, USA
$12

9. Klingon Make-up Kit

Rubie's, USA, 1994
$25

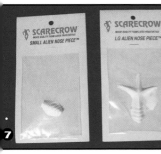

Uniform/Kleidung

1. Boxer Shorts

pure silk, with communicator motif
RM style
$25
(After Capt. Sisko introduced them on DS9,
Chakotay and Tom Paris are said to have
been seen in these.)

2. Boxer Shorts

pure silk
with communicator motif
RM style
$25
(Revealed on washday in DS9; now we
finally know what Julian wears underneath.)

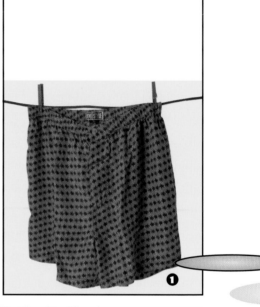

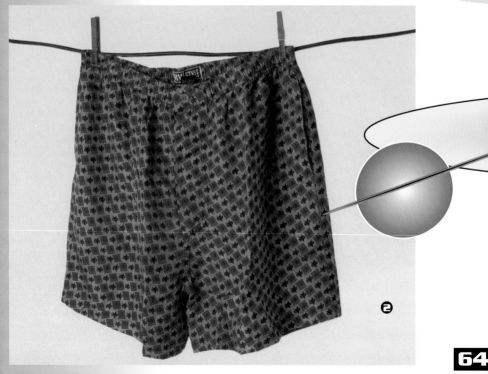

3

3. Baseball Cap with Ferengi Emblem
Cotton. P.P.C., USA, 1994
$25

4. Baseball Cap with "UFP Starfleet HQ" Emblem
simple version
$15

4

5

5. Baseball Cap with "Starfleet Academy"
Multicolor embroidery on cotton
P.P.C., USA, 1996
$23

2. T-shirt: "The Team for Tomorrow"

T-shirt is a parody of slogans from United States' presidential campaigns
$30

3. T-shirt with "Starfleet Academy XXL Phys. Ed. Dept."

Stanley Desantes, 1996
$18

1. Outfit for Medical Personnel

"Starfleet Medical Unit"
$30

4. Ship and DS9 Contour
5. McCoy, Spock, and Kirk
6. Spock: "Live long and prosper"
7. Picard
8. Ships of Action
9. Voyager
10. Enterprise A

All ties by
Ralph Marlin, USA
$25

1. Classic Episode Pin
"The Lights of Zetar"
$12

2. Classic Enterprise 1701 Pin
$10

3. Classic Star Trek Pin
$10

4. Classic Star Trek Pin
multicolor embroidery
$18

5. Classic Klingon Emblem Pin
$10

6. Classic Vulcan IDIC Emblem
Symbolizes "infinite diversity in infinite combinations"
$10

All pins in this chapter, unless otherwise indicated, were made by Hollywood Pins, USA

7. Classic Command Symbol

keyring
P.P.C., USA
$10

8. Classic Enterprise 1701

keyring
P.P.C., USA
$12

9. UFP — Starfleet HQ

embroidered cloth sew-on patch
P.P.C., USA
$6

10. Classic Emblem "Engineering"

sew-on patch
P.P.C., USA, 1980
$5

11. Classic Emblem "Medical Personnel"

sew-on patch
P.P.C., USA, 1980 $5

12. Classic Emblem "Science"

sew-on patch
P.P.C., USA, 1980 $5

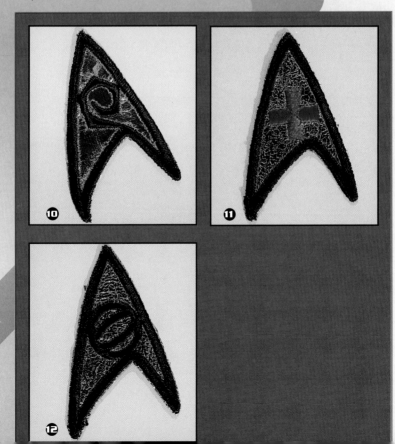

PINS/SCHMUCK

1. The Movies — Uniform Belt Buckle

heavy brass version
$18

2. The Movies — Fleet Admiral's Insignia

$15

3. The Movies — Admiral's Insignia

$15

4. The Movies — Captain's Insignia

$15

5. The Movies — One-year Service Pin

P.P.C., USA
6 DM

6. The Movies — Five-year Service Pin

P.P.C., USA
$4

6a. The Movies — 10-year Service Pin

P.P.C., USA
$4

7. The Movies — Shoulder Stripes Back Pin

P.P.C., USA, 1979
$12

8. The Movies — Uniform Emblem

cast brass, enameled, gilded
Original from film
Gift from Majel Barrett-Roddenberry
value cannot be estimated

9. The Movies — Uniform Emblem

enameled, gilded
P.P.C., USA, 1987
ca, $65

10. The Movies — Commodore's Insignia

Original from film
Gift from Majel Barrett-Roddenberry
value cannot be estimated

11. The Movies — Uniform Belt Buckle

Original from the film
Gift from Majel Barrett-Roddenberry
value cannot be estimated

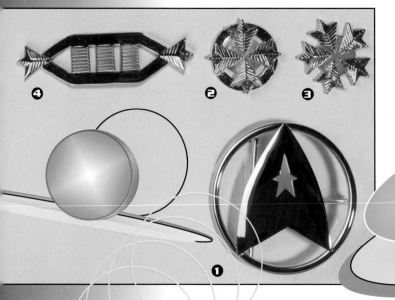

8

6

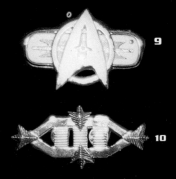

9

6a   **5**

7

10

11

1. Classic U.S.S. Enterprise Pin
$10

2. Classic Command Symbol Pin
$10

3. Classic Science Symbol Pin
$16

4. Classic U.S.S. Enterprise NCC 1701
multicolored enamel, $12

5. Starfleet Command Communication Pin
$10

6. Delegation & Visitor ID Cards
Earth Delegation, Vulcan Delegation, Visitor
Creation Convention cards
USA, 1992, $6 each

7. Classic keyring: "Live long and prosper"
The Hollywood Pin, USA
$12

8. Classic Arcaria Logo keyring
Diecast, enameled
Rawcliffe, USA, 1994: $20

9. Classic Tricorder keyring
Diecast motif
Rawcliffe, USA, 1994: $12

10. Star Trek 30-years Pin
$10

11. Star Trek 30-years Pin
$10

12. Star Trek 30-years Pin
$10

13. Star Trek Generations Pin
$12

14. Voyager Ship Pin
$12

15. VOY 1995 Cast & Crew Pin
$12

other pins by The Hollywood Pins, USA.

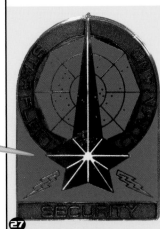

PINS/SCHMUCK

**1. DS9
VOY Communicator**

alternative version, slightly different shape

Thayer's Jewellery, USA $20

**2. DS9 matte
VOY Communicator**

Hollywood Pins, USA, 1996 $15

3. Commander's Rank Pin

P.P.C., USA, 1996 $12

4. Lieutenant's Rank Pin

P.P.C., USA, 1996 $12

5. Bat'telh keyring

Rawcliffe, USA, 1995 $12

6. Galaxy Class Spaceship keyring

Rawcliffe, USA, 1994 $12

7. TNG "U.S.S. Enterprise" Sticker

Rends International, Canada $2

8. Enterprise 1701 Sew-on Patch

$10

9. Star Trek 25th Anniversary Sew-on Patch

$12

10. Star Trek 25th Anniversary Pin

$15

11. Peace in Our Galaxy Pin

$10

12. United Federation of Planets Pin

$10

13. Romulan Symbol Pin

$10

14. Star Trek 25-years Pin

$6

15. Star Trek 25-years Pin with Spaceship

$12

16. Vulcan Greeting Pin

$12

17. Enterprise 1701 Pin

gilded in 14-karat gold
value not known

18. "Engage" Pin

The Hollywood Pins, USA
$12

19. Star Trek TNG Silver-colored Pin

The Hollywood Pins, USA
$12

20. Klingon Communicator Pin

The Hollywood Pins, USA
$18

21. Ferengi Script keyring

$12

22. Cardassian Symbol keyring

$12

23. Klingon Dagger keyring

$12

24. Starfleet Academy keyring

$12

25. UFP Symbol keyring

$12

26. Maquis Symbol keyring

The Hollywood Pins, USA
$12

27. Bajoran Emblem keyring

$12

28. Star Trek V The Final Frontier Pin

$12

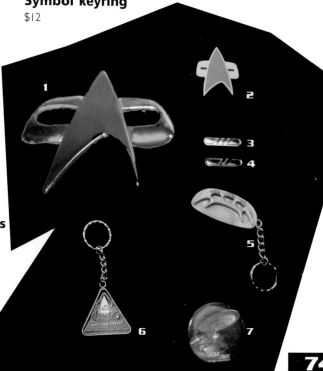

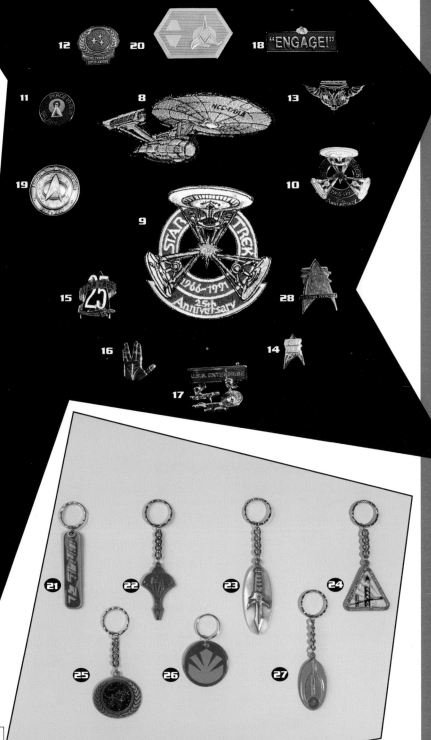

12
20
18 "ENGAGE!"
11
8 NCC-1701-A
13
19
10
9 STAR TREK 1966-1991 25th Anniversary
15
28
16
14
17 U.S.S. ENTERPRISE
21
22
23
24
25
26
27

❶

❷

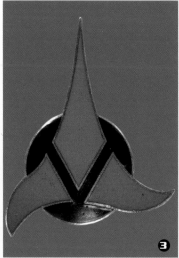

❸

❹

1. Cardassian Symbol Pin

$11

2. Generations Promotion Pin

given away at film premier
P.P.C., USA, 1994
value not known

3. Klingon Logo Pin (old)

$10

4. Communicator Pin

Sat1 Promotion, 1995
was given away

5. TNG "The Inner Light" Episode Pin

$15

6. TNG Klingon Pin

$7

7. UFP Symbol Pin

$10

8. TNG Locutus of Borg Pin

$12

9. TNG "Yesterday's Enterprise" Pin

$15

10. TNG Starfleet Academy Pin

$10

11. Borg Symbol keyring

$9

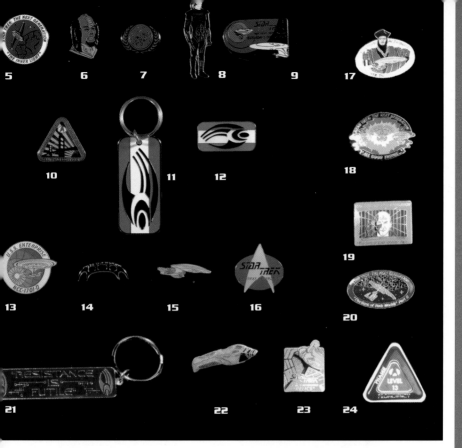

12. TNG Borg Symbol Pin
$10
13. TNG Enterprise 1701 D Pin
$12
14. TNG Klingon Bat'telh Pin
$10
15. TNG Enterprise 1701-D Pin
$10
16. Star Trek The Next Generation Pin
$10
17. TNG "Encounter at Farpoint" Episode Pin
$15
18. TNG "Relics" Episode Pin
$15

19. TNG "Best of Both Worlds I" Episode Pin
$15
20. TNG "Best of Both Worlds II" Episode Pin
$15
21. "Resistance is futile" keyring
$10
22. TNG Phaser Pin
$10
23. TNG "All good things" Episode Pin
$15
24. TNG "Phaser Range 13" Sharpshooter Pin
$9

Made by The Hollywood Pins, USA

1. DS9 Quark's Bar Pin

$12

2. DS9 "The Emissary" Episode Pin

$12

3. DS9 Cardassian Destroyer Pin

$15

4. DS9 Cast & Crew 1994-95 Pin

$12

5. DS9 Defiant Pin

$12

6. DS9 1993 Season Pin

$12

7. DS9 Station Pin

$10

9. Bajoran Communicator

diecast, painted, bought at a convention
maker unknown
$15

10. Bajoran Rank Pins

See drawing for ranks; P.P.C., USA, 1995
$7 each

11. DS9 Runabout Pin

The Hollywood Pins, USA
$15

12. Star Trek DS9 Pin

The Hollywood Pins, USA
$12

13. DS9-VOY Communicator Pin

The Hollywood Pins, USA
small $5,
medium $9
large $15

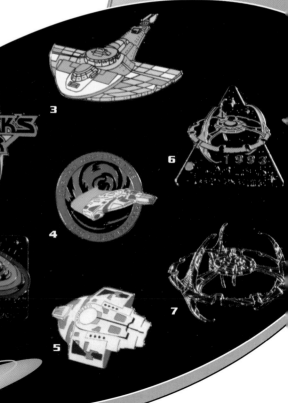

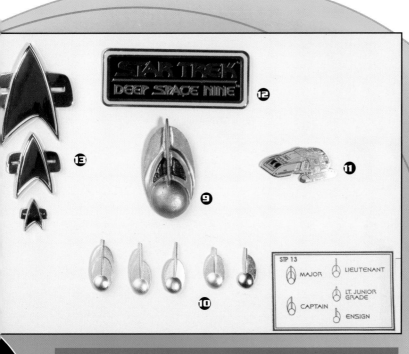

STP 13

MAJOR   LIEUTENANT

LT. JUNIOR
GRADE

CAPTAIN   ENSIGN

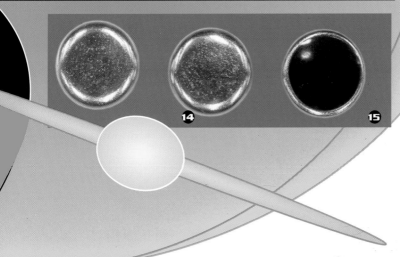

14. Rank Pins

gold-colored metal; P.P.C., USA
$3 each

15. Rank Pins

gold-colored metal, black
with gold rim
P.P.C., USA
$3 each

1

Official Communicator Pin
With Authentic Sound!

COMMUNICATOR
SOUNDBOARD™

GIVE YOUR
COMMUNICATOR

2

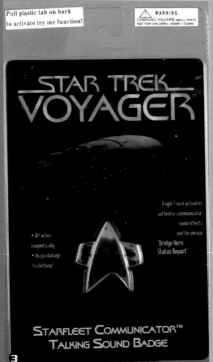

STAR TREK
VOYAGER™

A light touch activates
authentic communicator
sound effects
and the phrase
"Bridge Here
Status Report"

• Attaches
magnetically
• No pin damage
to clothing!

STARFLEET COMMUNICATOR™
TALKING SOUND BADGE

3

Close-up view of the VOY communicator

1. TNG Communicator

plastic, with original sound
battery powered
Köhn Inc., 1994 $12

2. Communicator Soundboard

to complete metal communicator
battery powered
authentic sound $12

3. VOY Communicator

sticks to clothing magnetically
battery powered, with sound and voice:
"Bridge here, Status Report"
IPI, USA, 1996 $17

4. Bajoran Communicator

sticks to clothing magnetically
battery powered
with sound and voice:
"OPS here, go ahead!"
IPI, USA, 1996 $17

5. Klingon Communicator

sticks to clothing magnetically
battery powered, with sound and Klingon voice
IPI, USA, 1996 $17

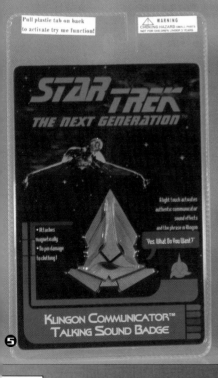

PINS/SCHMUCK

❷

❸

1. Star Trek Wristwatch

Limited edition
with Fossil certificate
price not known

Close-up of Fossil watch
with package

2. TNG Chrono Scanner

Timex, USA
no longer made. $55

3. TNG Klingon Watch

Timex, USA;
no longer made. $55

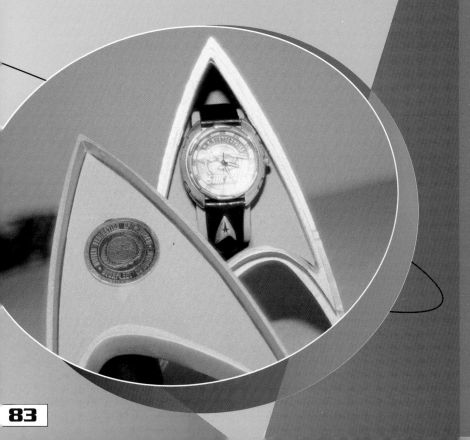

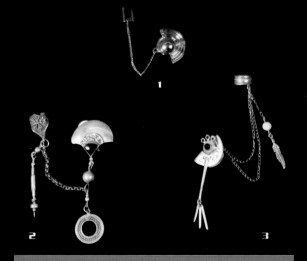

1. Major Kira's Earring

with clip or pin
P.P.C., USA, 1994
$18

2. Bajoran Earring

"Ring and Bar," single piece
925 Sterling silver
Value of material:
about $38

3. Bajoran Earring

"Pearl and Feather," single piece
925 Sterling silver
Value of material:
about $25

4. Bajoran Earring

925 Sterling silver
Sabine Tirpitz, Munich
$20

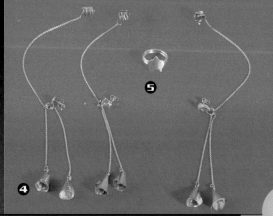

5. Communicator Ring

925 Sterling silver
Sabine Tirpitz, Munich
$30

6. Romulan "Bird of Prey"

large brass piece, gilded
Thayer's Jewellery, USA
$38

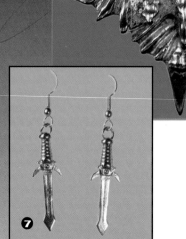

7. TNG Klingon swords

Earrings
The Hollwood Pins, USA
$17

Props

Employees of moving-picture companies or theaters call any functional thing that's not a part of the theater or film set's scenery or decoration, a "prop." More formally, these things are known as "stage properties."

Typical movie props simulate items one would find in a typical environment, real-life goods such as cups or books. But classic Star Trek props have attempted to "simulate" something that either doesn't exist, such as tricorders, or things too risky to use safely, such as weapons.

Thus a lot of items have come onto the market for the Star Trek fan over the years, from accurate but non-functioning models to electronic toys with light and sound effects, everything imaginable.

Some of these "props" are shown on the following pages.

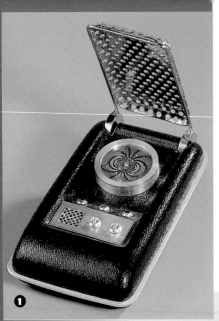

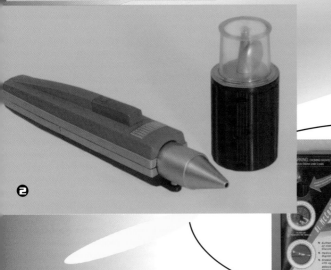

1. Classic Communicator

exactly identical to the original in
size and shape
Single piece, presumably a kit
from the '70s
Maker and value unknown

2. Dr. McCoy's Medical Kit

Medical scanner with sound and skin
regenerator
Battery powered, with lights
$25
(Ideal for live role-players, with diploma
from the Starfleet Medical Academy for the
doctor in question — fill it out, frame it,
and it's yours!)

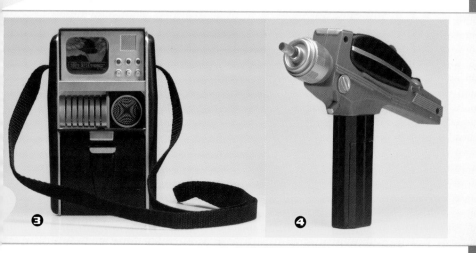

3. Classic Tricorder

battery powered
with lit, fold-out screen,
diodes, and two different
scanner sounds
$30

4. Classic Phaser

battery powered
with controlled "ray" (light)
firing sounds
$30

5. Classic Communicator

battery powered, with 3-second
recording and playback functions
for one's own commands
$38

6. Tribble

grunts and squeaks
(with battery)
Starstruck, USA, 1991
$28
*Never expose it to bright light or get it
wet! Don't feed it after midnight! And
never give it to a Klingon! (or anything
similar...)*

Unless otherwise noted, all articles are
made by Playmates-Bandai, USA.

PROPS

1. Movie Phaser

battery powered with two firing sounds, lights, and side belt clip
$30

2. Movie Communicator

battery operated,
lit screen,
three signal sounds
$30

4. "The Phoenix" Dagger

stainless steel
with folding side blades
leather scabbard.
33 centimeters long
riveted no-slip wooden handle
United, USA, 1991
$125
("May you die well"
— old Klingon saying)

5. "Combat" Dagger

straight type, stainless steel,
leather scabbard
33 mm long, riveted
no-slip wooden handle
Haller, Germany
$60

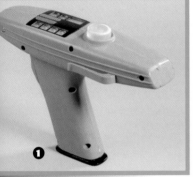

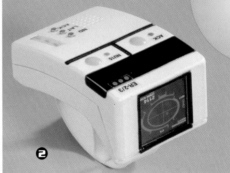

3. Klingon Disruptor

battery powered
lit point
two firing sounds
no longer made
original price $30

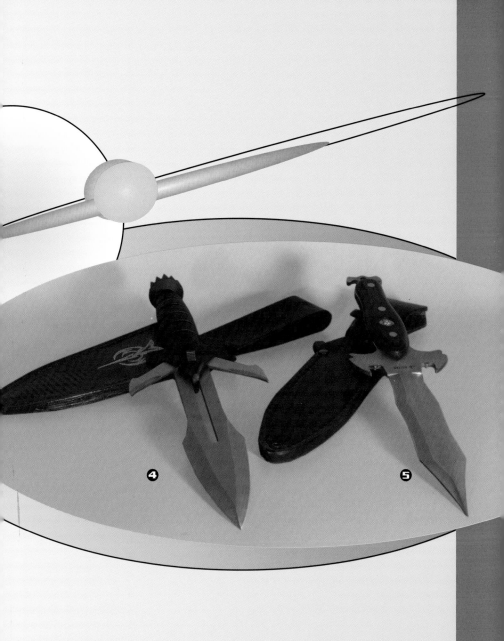

4

5

Unless otherwise noted, all articles
are made by Playmates-Bandai, USA

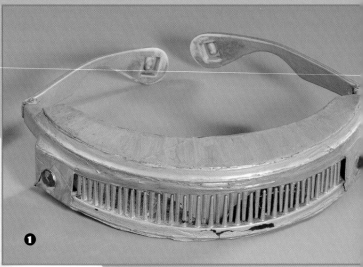

1. Visor

hair clip with sides of bicycle glasses,
plastic, paint, two rhinestones
made for Munich Trek dinner
material worth $12

3. TNG Phaser Type 1

keyring, battery powered, with light and
shot signs

4. TNG Soundboard

keyring, battery powered, with eight
different sounds (phaser, transporter,
door, etc.)

5. Classic Communicator

keyring, battery powered, with blinking
light and call signal when opened

IPI, USA, 1995
$14

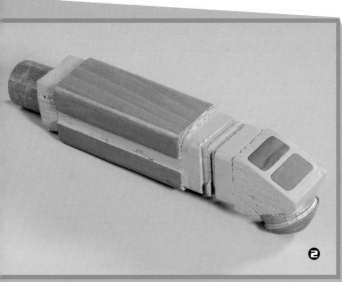

2. Hypospray with replace- able cartridge

Various pre-finished wooden pieces, glue, paint;
made by Daniela Hörl
for Munich Trek dinner
material worth $10

6. TNG Mini Tricorder

keyring, battery-powered
blinks and beeps

7 TOS Mini Phaser

keyring, battery powered, with light and
firing sounds
IPI, USA, 1995
$14

8. Eye of the Borg Crosis

battery powered
electronic stick-on pin
Chrysalid Group, Inc., 1995
$18

9. Lieutenant Worf's Klingon Medallions

Chrysalid Group, Inc., 1995
$18

1. TNG Phaser Type 1

battery powered, with light and two firing sounds
no longer produced; original price $30

2. TNG Phaser Type 2

("Cobrahead") battery powered, with light and two firing sounds
no longer produced; original price $30

3. TNG Tricorder

with lit screen, running light,
and three different scanning sounds
no longer produced; original price $30

4. Hypospray with replaceable cartridge

metal and plastic; made by an unknown fan
obtained at a convention; $30

5. DS9 PADD (Personal Access Data Display)

accurate scale model, each a single piece
Marc Tacke, Germany
material worth $30

6. TNG PADD

the somewhat larger version

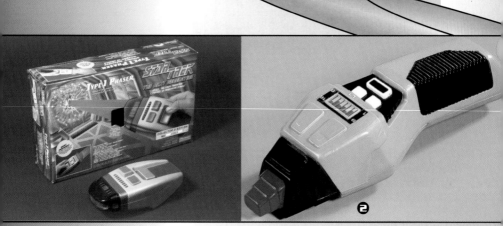

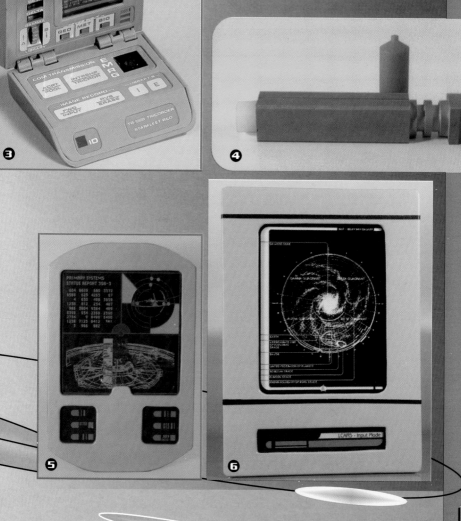

PROPS

Unless otherwise noted, all articles were made by Playmates-Bandai, USA.

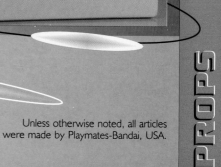

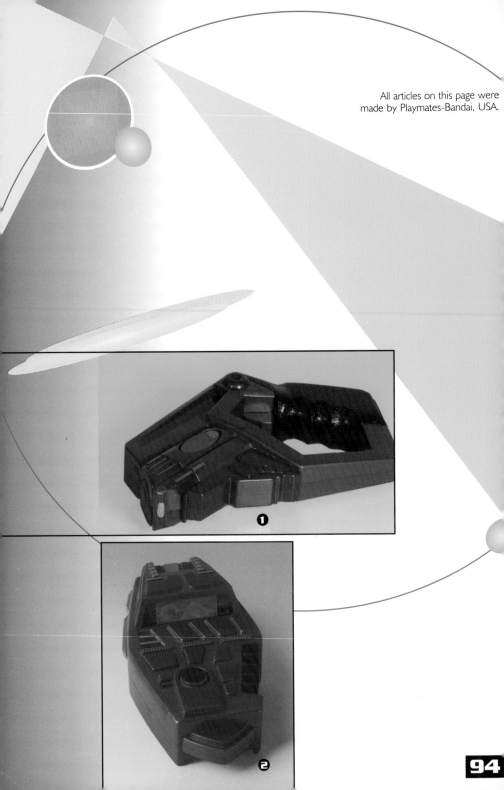

All articles on this page were made by Playmates-Bandai, USA.

94

1. Bajoran Phaser

battery-powered with light and shot sounds
no longer produced
original price $30

2. DS9 Bajoran Tricorder

battery powered, with lit screen and 3 different scanning sounds
no longer produced
original price $30

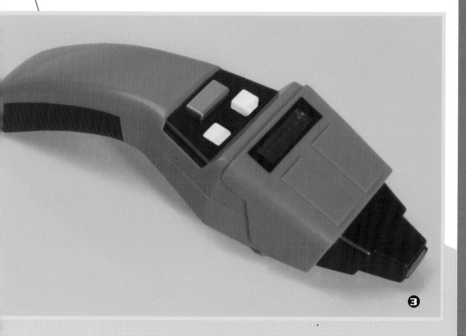

3. First Contact Phaser

battery powered, with light and 2 different firing sounds
$30

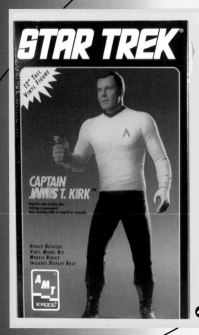

1

2

3

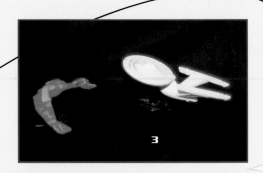

4

5

1. "Classic" Bridge Model Kit

diameter 31 centimeters
AMT, 1980
$15

2. Classic Enterprise

with light and 2 different sound effects
size 40 centimeters
Playmates-Bandai, USA
$75

3. Classic Enterprise & Klingon Bird of Prey

metal miniatures, Matchbox, GB, 1980
value not known

4. Captain Kirk Model Kit

AMT-Ertl, 1995
$40

5. Mr. Spock Model Kit

AMT-Ertl, 1995
$40

6. Classic Enterprise

25th anniversary edition
large model
limited to 2,000 pieces
Franklin Mint, USA, 1991
$490

7. Close-up of Model 6

(with open bridge)

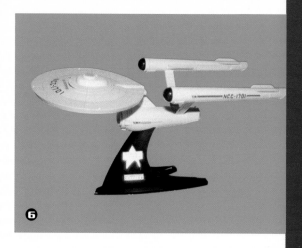

6

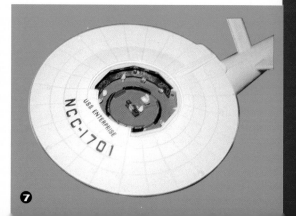

7

MODELLE

1

2

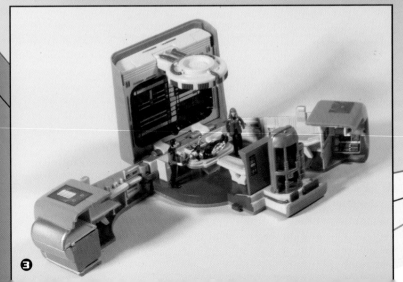

3

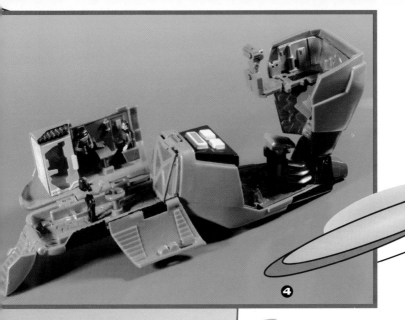

④

1. Inner Space Shuttle
$18

2. Inner Space Borg Cube
$18

3. Inner Space Medical Tricorder
no longer produced
original price $25

4. Inner Space Phaser Type II
no longer produced
Original price $25

Playmates-Bandai, USA

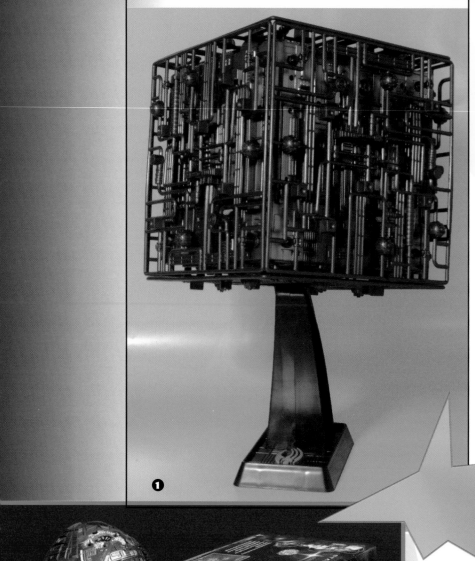

1

2

1. Borg Cube

with light and 3 different sound effects
$80

2. Borg Sphere

with light and 3 different sound effects
battle damage can be inserted or removed
$75

3. TNG Enterprise D

battery powered, with light and 4 different sound effects
$60

4. TNG Enterprise D
Transwarping

(variable plastic model)
$45

Playmates-Bandai, USA

MODELLE

101

1. Micro Machine Mobile

Value of materials
worth $155
*(With some creativity, one can make
something like this of Micro Machines.)*

2. TOS Micro Machines
Enterprise 1701

Ideal
$4

3. TNG Micro Machines
U.S.S. Stargazer

Ideal
$4

4. TOS Micro Machines

Botany Bay
Klingon Battlecruiser
Romulan Bird of Prey
Ideal
$12

5. DS9 Micro Machines

Space Station DS9
Cardassian Galor Warship
Runabout
Ideal
$12

6. TNG Micro Machines

Vulcan Shuttle Surak
U.S.S. Grissom
U.S.S. Excelsior
Ideal
$12

7. TNG Micro Machines

Borg Ship
Ferengi Marauder
U.S.S. Enterprise C
Ideal
$12

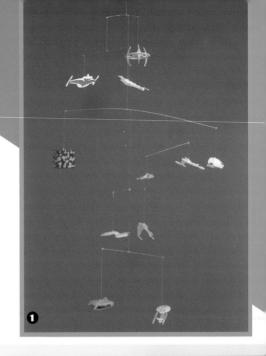

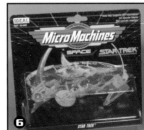

8. Micro Machines Star Trek Limited Edition Collector's Set II

containing items from
the episode *All Good Things*:
U.S.S. Enterprise D (3 power plants), U.S.S. Pasteur, Klingon Battlecruiser
From other episodes:
Shuttle Galileo II, Space Station K-7, Botany Bay, U.S.S. Enterprise C, U.S.S. Stargazer,
Romulan Scout Ship, U.S.S. Defiant, U.S.S. Enterprise B, U.S.S. Enterprise D (separable),
U.S.S. Farragut, Vulcan Shuttle Sarek,
Federation Space Dock, U.S.S. Grissom

Galoob Toys, Inc., USA
The ships from *All Good Things* are available only in this set,
numbered collector's edition in presentation cases.

$55

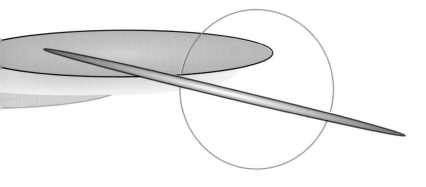

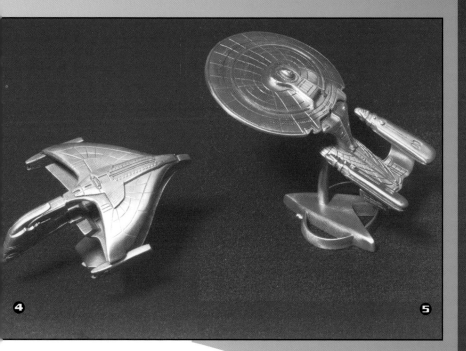

1. Limited edition
U.S.S. Grissom

metal miniature,
Rawcliffe, USA, 1991
$26

2. Limited edition Regula I
Space Laboratory

metal miniature
Rawcliffe, USA, 1991
$35

3. Klingon Battlecruiser

limited edition
Rawcliffe, USA, 1991
$25

4. Limited edition
Romulan Warbird

metal miniature, limited edition
Rawcliffe, USA, 1992
$50

5. Limited edition
Enterprise 1701-D

metal miniature
can be separated
Rawcliffe, USA, 1994
$75

6. Kazon Fighter Kit

printed in color
Revell, 1996
$3

7. Voyager Kit

printed in color
Revell, 1996
$3

8. Maquis
Fighter Kit

printed in color
Revell, 1996
$3

MODELLE

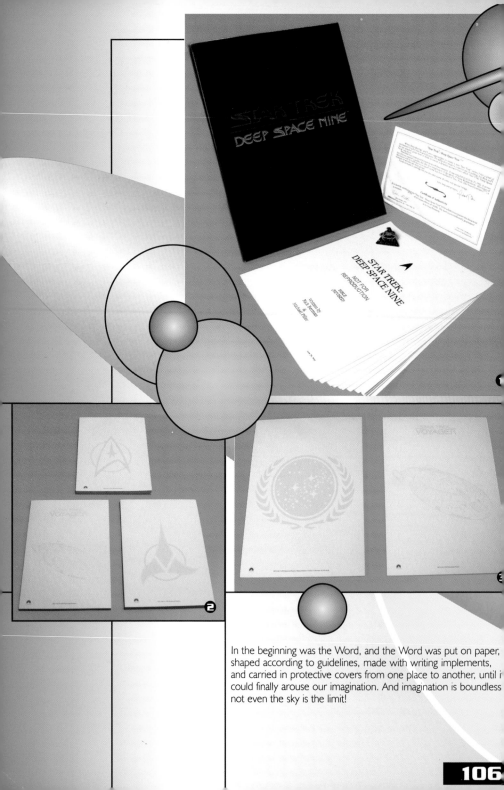

In the beginning was the Word, and the Word was put on paper, shaped according to guidelines, made with writing implements, and carried in protective covers from one place to another, until it could finally arouse our imagination. And imagination is boundless, not even the sky is the limit!

⑤

⑥

1. DS9 Writer's Bible

with certificate and pin
limited edition, 10,000 pieces
Berman & Piller
$18
"In the beginning was the Word"

2. Writing Pad A5

Classic Command Symbol
Filmwelt Berlin, 1996
$7
Voyager Symbol
Filmwelt Berlin, 1996
$7
Klingon Symbol
Filmwelt Berlin, 1996
$7

3. Writing Pad A4

UFP Symbol
Filmwelt Berlin, 1996
$8
Voyager Symbol
Filmwelt Berlin, 1996
$8

4. Plastic Case with Starfleet Command Emblem

P.P.C., USA
$12

5. Space Pen

silver and black
Fisher Space Pen Co., USA
$38
(These pens not only look good but really write
in any conditions, even under water, over grease
and oil, upside down, and in gravity-free
situations. If need be, one can even repair real
space ships with them, as was proven on an
American lunar expedition, when an important
switch broke off and was brought back into
operation with a pen cap.)

6. Back of writing pad shown at left

(The backs of the A5 pads include two postcards,
those of the A4 pads have four postcards.)

MEDIEN

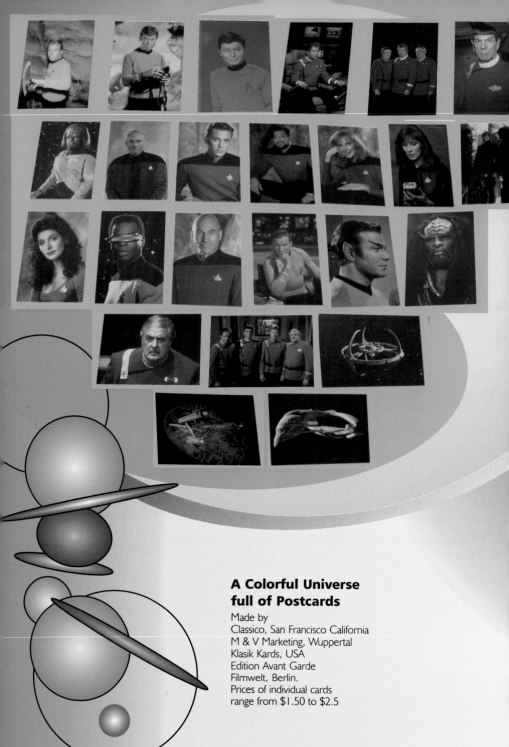

A Colorful Universe full of Postcards

Made by
Classico, San Francisco California
M & V Marketing, Wuppertal
Klasik Kards, USA
Edition Avant Garde
Filmwelt, Berlin.
Prices of individual cards
range from $1.50 to $2.5

MEDIEN

1. Star Trek VI
The Undiscovered Country
Movie Cards
eight large photos from the film,
édition trèves
$30

2 Star Trek DS9 TV Cards
eight large photos from the series
collector's edition, 1993
$30

3. Star Trek TNG TV Cards
eight large photos from the series
collector's edition, 1992
$30

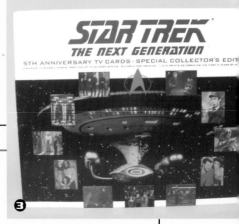

4. TNG "Locutus of Borg" Postcard

5. TNG "Hugh Borg" Postcard

Portico Desing, USA, 1994
$2

6. Visions of the Final Frontier

Art Portfolio (art prints of drawings and graphics)
Star Struck, USA, 1991
$30

Heineken. Refreshes the parts other beers cannot reach.

"The vulgar, beer-guzzling Vulcan"

The bold title said: "Heineken. Refreshes the parts other beers cannot reach.
A familiar voice whispered in my ear:
Spock: "What does it mean?"
Nimoy: "It's an advertisement to sell beer."
Spock: "I am not sure if I completely understand its meaning. "Refreshes the parts other beers cannot reach? My ears, for example? Is this an attempt at humor?"
Nimoy: "It's a joke, Spock, with a sexual subtext."
Spock: "Ah. (pause) Not exactly what I would call a dignified presentation in so public a place. Did you authorize this?"
Nimoy: "No! Certainly not! It's a giant pain in the ass."
Spock: "A strange place for the discomfort to manifest itself."
Nimoy: "It's a figure of speech, Spock. Let me deal with this."
Spock: "Please do."

From *I am Spock*, Leonard Nimoy's autobiography, German edition by Heyne, 1997.

1. Heineken "Spock" Poster

Heineken Brewery
London, 1978.
$12

2. "No Escape" Greeting Card

PopShots, USA
$6

3. "Locutus of Borg"
Greeting Card

PopShots, USA
$6

4. Cardboard Figures

Geordie LaForge, William Riker,
Dr. Beverly Crusher, and Worf
Portico Design, USA, 1995
$6

5. 1701-D Postcard
stands up

Portico Design, USA, 1995
$6

1. Star Trek TOS 1995 Calendar
Pocket Books, USA, 1994
$12

2. Star Trek TOS 1994 Calendar
Pocket Books, USA, 1993
$12

3. Gold Stamp from ST Generations Stamp Collection Series
limited edition, 50,000 pieces
in display case
with first-day cover and certificate
SSCA, USA, 1994
value not known

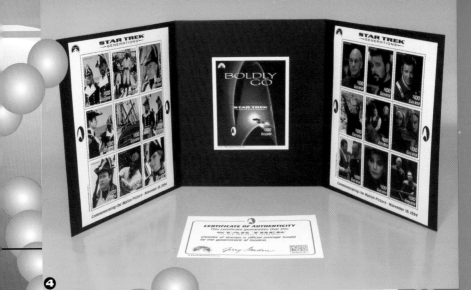

4. ST Generations Stamp Collection

limited edition with certificate.
These stamps could really be used
on letters sent in French Guiana.
SSCA, USA, 1994
value not known

5. First-day Covers from ST Generations Stamp Collection Series

limited edition with certificate
SSCA, USA, 1994
value not known

1

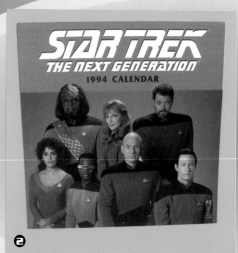

2

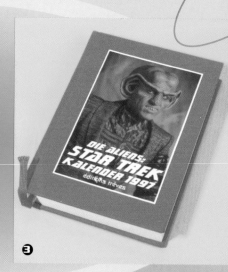

3

1. Visions 1997 Calendar

The Worlds of Tobias J. Richter
Heel Verlag, 1996
$18
(At last Tobias's wonderful digital worlds can be hung on the wall!)

2. Star Trek TNG 1994 Calendar

Pocket Books, USA, 1993
$12

3. Star Trek Calendar 1997:
The Aliens

édition trèves, 1996
$12

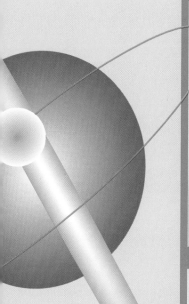

4. Star Trek TNG
1995 Calendar

Pocket Books, USA, 1994
$12

5. Star Trek DS9
1995 Calendar

Pocket Books, USA, 1994
$12

MEDIEN

1

2

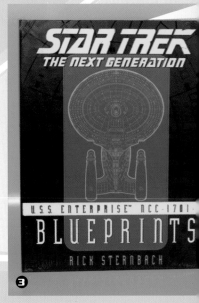

3

1. U.S.S. Excelsior Blueprints

Mastercom Data Center, USA, 1996
$20

2. Blueprint Collection

TOS, TNG, DS, Zanart Entertainment Inc., USA, 1994
$28

3. Enterprise 1701-D Blueprints

Rick Sternbach, Pocket Books, USA
$40

4. Spaceship and Space Station Blueprints

Lawrence Miller
$20

1. *Star Trek Communicator*
Klingon issue
official Star Trek Fan Club magazine
USA, 1995
$4

2. *Star Trek: The Official Monthly Magazine*
September 1995
Titan Magazines, London, 1995
$5

3. *Star Trek: The Official Monthly Magazine*
May 1995
Titan Magazines, London, 1995
$5

4. *The Trekker*
Fan Magazine
three issues shown.
Cosmic Dolphin Inc., USA, 1996
$8

①

②

③

④

1. ST: DS9 — The Official Magazine

Number 6
Starlog, USA, 1994
$9

2. ST: DS9 — The Official Magazine

Number 8
Starlog, USA, 1994
$9

⑤

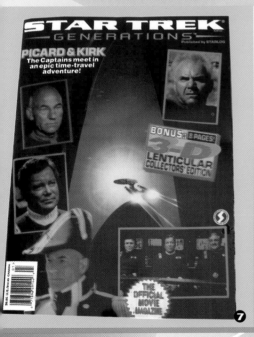

3. *ST: Der Erste Kontakt*
Book on film *First Contact*
German edition
Punchline Publishing Inc., 1996
$5.50

4. *ST: DS9* — **The Official Magazine**
Number 9
Starlog, USA, 1994
$9

5. *Starlog* **20th Anniversary**
special edition
USA 1996
$12

6. *Cinefantastique*
1991
$12

7. *Star Trek Generations*
The Official Movie Magazine
limited edition
with 3-D cover
Starlog, USA, 1994
$14

MEDIEN

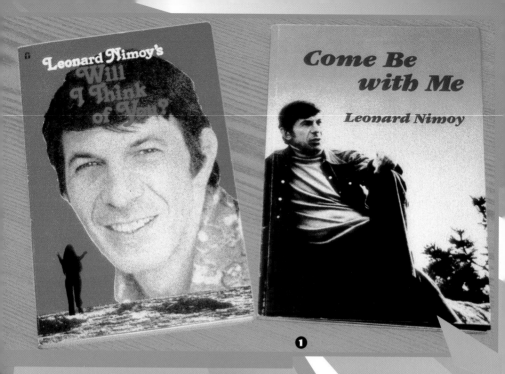

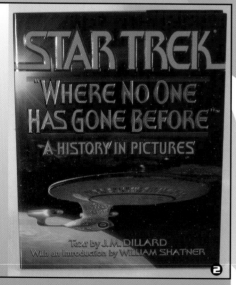

1. Leonard Nimoy's Early Books

stories and poems; rarities

2. *Star Trek: Where No One Has Gone Before*

A history in pictures.
J. M. Dillard
Pocket Books, USA
$45

3. The first page of the Roddenberry biography

4. *Star Trek Creator*

Gene Roddenberry's authorized biography
David Alexander
Pocket Books, USA

To Gene Roddenberry,
who proved Ghandi was right.
One man can shake the world gently.

His Vision Lives
May H Barrett
Roddenberry

❸

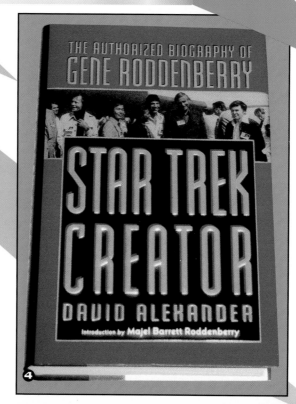

THE AUTHORIZED BIOGRAPHY OF
GENE RODDENBERRY

STAR TREK
CREATOR

DAVID ALEXANDER

Introduction by Majel Barrett Roddenberry

❹

MEDIEN

1. *Lost Voyages of Trek and the Next Generation*

(About manuscripts not yet filmed or shown.)
E. Gross & M. A. Altmann
Boxtree, London, 1995
$20

2. *Why You Should Never Beam Down in a Red Shirt*

Robert W. Bly
Harper Perennial
$14

3. *To The Stars*

George Takei's autobiography
Pocket Books, USA
$15

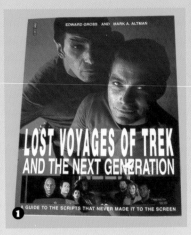

4. *The Klingon Dictionary*

Marc Okrand
Pocket Books, USA $15

5. *The Physics of Star Trek*

Lawrence M. Krauss
Pocket Books, USA $25

6. *Star Trek Concordance*

BJO Trimble
Citadel Press, USA, 1995 $20

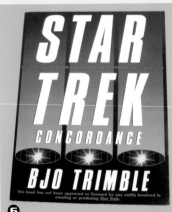

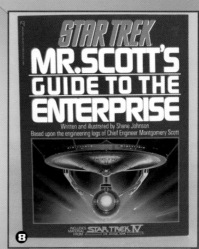

7. *Starfleet Uniform Recognition Manual*

Shane Johnson
The Noron Group, USA, 1985
$15
(Recommended for all hobby
tailors who can use detailed
uniform drawings with
information on colors.)

8. *Mr. Scott's Guide to the Enterprise*

Shane Johnson
Pocket Books, USA, 1987
$20
(a lovingly illustrated detailed guide
through the Enterprise)

9. *U.S.S. Enterprise Officer's Manual*

Starfleet Publication Office, USA
$20

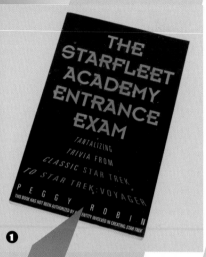

1

2

3

4

1. *The Starfleet Academy Entrance Exam*

Peggy Robin
Citadel Press, USA, 1996
$15

2. *Star Trek: First Contact*

J. M. Dillard
Pocket Books, USA, 1996
$30

3. *Creating the Next Generation*

E. Gross, M. A. Altmann
Boxtree, London, 1995
$25

4. *Star Trek: The Klingon Way*

A Warrior's Guide
Mark Orkrand
Pocket Books, USA, 1996
$15

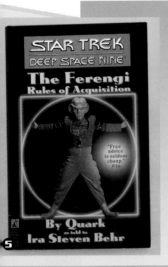

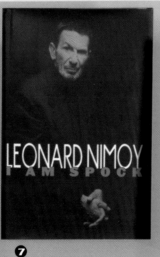

5. *The Ferengi Rules of Acquisition*

By Quark, as told to Ira Steven Behr
Pocket Books, USA, 1995
$8

6. *The Nitpicker's Guide for Classic Trekkers*

Phil Farrand
Pocket Books, USA
$15

7. *I Am Spock*

Leonard Nimoy's autobiography
Hyperion, USA
$30

MEDIEN

1

2

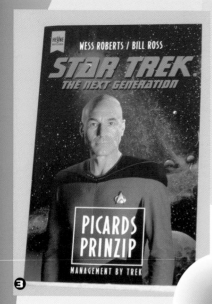

3

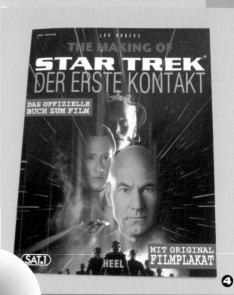

4

1. Inside Star Trek
The Real Story
H. F. Solow & R. H. Justmann
Pocket Books, USA
$40

2. Die Entstehung
der Trek Filme
(*The Origin of the Trek Films*),
edited by Edward Gross
VGS, Germany
$18

3. Picards Prinzip
(*Picard's Principle*)
Management by Trek
W. Roberts & B. Ross
Heyne Verlag, Germany, 1996
$8

4. The Making
of Star Trek:
Der Erste Kontakt
Lou Anders
German edition
by Heel Verlag, 1996
$18

6. Das Offizielle
Wörterbuch
Klingonisch-Deutsch
(*Klingon-German Dictionary*)
by Mark Okrand
Heel Verlag, Germany, 1996
$15

7. ST: Die Welten
der Föderation
(*The Worlds of the Federation*),
by Shane Johnson, German
edition
by Heel Verlag, 1996
$18

131

MEDIEN

1. DS9 Bookmarks
Antioch Publishing Co., USA, 1993
$2.50 each

2. Classic Bookmarks
Antioch Publishing Co., USA, 1993
$2.50 each

3. TNG Bookmarks
Antioch Publishing Co., USA, 1993
$2.50 each

4. Data Gift Box
3 videocassettes
English originals
CIC Video
$70

5. The Star Trek Movies
Limited Edition Box
7 videos
widescreen and Dolby stereo
CIC Video, 1995
$105

1. 25th Anniversary Audio Collection

This CD edition includes: *The First Adventure*, *Strangers from the Sky*, and *Final Frontier*, read by Leonard Nimoy, James Doohan, and George Takei, with an introduction by William Shatner.
Simon & Schuster Audio, 1991
$45

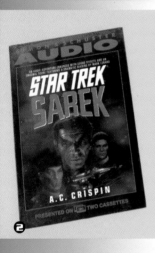

2. Star Trek: *Sarek*

Audio cassette from the original book by A. C. Crispin, read by Mark Lennard
Simon & Schuster Audio, 1994
$25

3. Star Trek TNG: *Kahless*

Audio cassette from the original book by M. J. Friedman, read by Kevin Conway
Simon & Schuster Audio, 1996
$25

4. Star Trek: *Prime Directive*

Audio cassette from the original book by Garfield and Judith Reeves Stevens, read by James Doohan
Simon & Schuster Audio, 1990
$25

5. Star Trek: *Generations*

Audio cassette from the original book by
J. M. Dillard, read by John DeLancie
Simon & Schuster Audio, 1994
$20

6. Star Trek: *Power Klingon*

Audio cassette from the original book by
B. Levine and M. Okrand, read by Michael
Dorn and Marc Okrand
Simon & Schuster Audio, 1993
$17
(The language course for Klingons and those
who want to "die well")

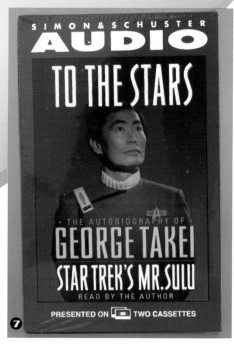

7. *To The Stars*

Audio cassette; George Takei reads
his autobiography
Simon & Schuster Audio, 1994
$20

MEDIEN

1. Laserdisc: Silver Anniversary

Laserdisc with holograms;
limited edition of
5,000 pieces
Starlog Press, USA, 1991
Original sale price $200

2. Laserdisc: Silver Anniversary

The same laserdisc, but with
this lighting the holograms
are not visible.

3. Star Trek: The Movie *Voyages*

The seven movies on laserdisc
special edition: widescreen and
Dolby stereo
Pioneer, USA
$305

4. Brent Spiner: *Ol' Yellow Eyes Is Back*

CD, Infinity Visions, 1994
$20

5. *Star Trek: Generations* Soundtrack

CD with computer clips
ZYX Music, 1994
$25

6. *Star Trek: First Contact* Soundtrack

CD with computer clips
ZYX Music, 1996
$25

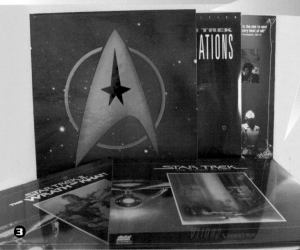

2

7

8

7. *Star Trek: DS9* Main Title
Maxi-CD
ZYX Music
$10

9

4

5

6

8. *Star Trek: Voyager* Main Title
Maxi-CD
ZYX Music $10

9. *Star Trek: 30th Anniversary Special*
CD
ZYX Music, 1996 $25

MEDIEN

1. *Star Trek: Omnipedia*

CD-ROM, voice-activated
Simon & Schuster Interactive
USA, 1995
$50

2. *Star Trek: Klingon*

CD-ROM, spoken by Jonathan Frakes and Robert O'Reilly.
This computer game can be played only by Klingons and such creatures as are fluent in the Klingon language or willing to learn it . . . ("Learn or die!")
Simon & Schuster Interactive
USA, 1996
$62

3. *Star Trek: Interactive Technical Manual*

CD-ROM, spoken by Jonathan Frakes and Majel
Barrett-Roddenberry
Simon & Schuster Interactive, USA, 1994
$45

4. Ambassador Sarek Mouse Pad

Mousetrak, USA, 1996
$13

5. "Captain Picard" Mouse Pad

Mousetrak, USA, 1996
$13

6. "Commander Riker" Mouse Pad

Mousetrak, USA, 1996
$20

7. *Star Trek: Warrior's Set*

Includes:
Technical Manual,
DS9 Harbinger Holodeck Mission,
CD-ROM,
Video, *The Way of the Warrior*, and
The Conventional Klingon CD
with language course
Viacom, USA
$55

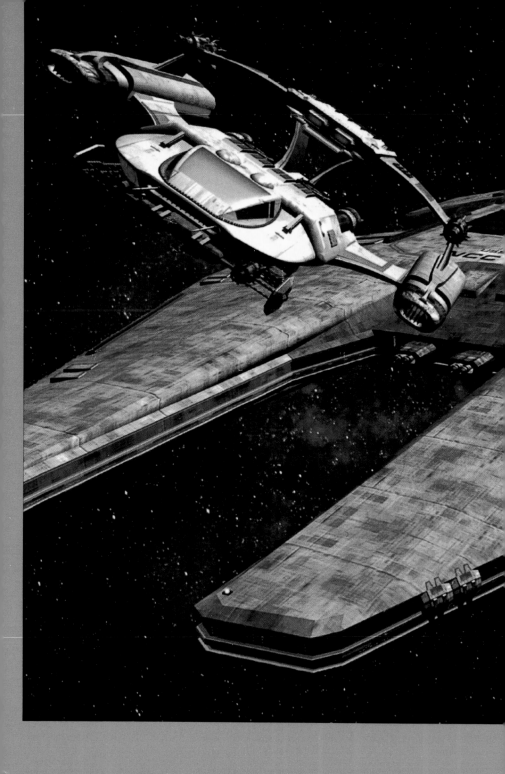

Trading Cards

Trading cards are not exactly new any more. They got their start in the 1950s in the United States with Topps baseball and football cards for all the major teams and their star athletes. At that time they were printed on sturdy cardboard — a good millimeter thick — either black and white or four-colored. Then, as now, they were packed in bundles of five, nine, or even fifteen individual cards. Only the most active trader and collector could assemble a complete set of them.

Some sets of cards, or single cards of sports stars, bring in a small fortune when sold at a collectors' meet. The sales strategy for trading cards is as simple as it is successful: A manufacturer selects any theme (such as Star Trek), assembles about ninety nice pictures with information about them, and has them printed. Then one separates the cards into small bundles — some images in most of the packs, some rarely included — and sells them to the fans. This worked in the 1950s and is no different today.

Trading cards are, so to speak, the "stamps" of the 1990s. Although they are not useful for anything, one can stick them into nice albums and look at them again and again. It is a very special fascination that can quickly become addictive.

I confess, I too am already infected by the trading-card virus and must force myself to sidestep certain series. This craving is especially serious among those who have fallen prey to the "special cards." This is also a specialty, with Etched Foil Cards, Foil-Embossed Cards, Chromium Cards, Holocards, Metalcards, Skymotion Cards, and many more.

What's the secret behind the success of the new card series? Very simply, in the last fifteen years, printing technology has improved by light years. Today it is possible to produce trading cards that look as though they were made of metal. Take the already legendary (and expensive!) Ship's Register Plates from *Reflections of the Future, Phase I*, for example. Or if we look at the development of holography, there are beautiful special cards with simple, doubled, or even more changeable motifs (such as ST:TNG Episode Collection, person cards or the cards of the "Holodoc" from the first Voyager series).

The Skymotion cards are also a genuine rarity. They can be had only in trade for an "Exchange Card." Exchange cards are put into the packages only in very small numbers (usually 1:72, one Exchange Card in 72 packages), or sold through chosen trading-card dealers, who generally charge upward of $65.

Skymotion cards are made of a thicker plastic material, similar to credit cards, and are transparent. When one looks at them in the light and changes the angle of the card, one sees the approximately 25 separate holograms of the card in series, like a short film.

Since there are many trading-card series in the Star Trek universe, we can, unfortunately, only touch upon this gigantic area of collecting, since we also want to present the Customizable Card Games on a few pages

Trading Cards

EVENT — STAR TREK THE NEXT GENERATION

ENGAGE SHUTTLE OPERATIONS

Most major starships are outfitted with shuttle hangars and equipment necessary to launch and recover shuttlecraft.

Plays on table. Shuttlecraft may be carried and launched from your ships (if tractor beams and ENGINEER present) AND land on planets (requires their total RANGE).

DILEMMA — STAR TREK THE NEXT GENERATION

EMPATHIC ECHO

In 2370, following the suicide of partially empathic Lt. Daniel Kwan, Deanna Troi experienced visions of a past murder, reliving it through the participants' eyes.

One personnel present with Empathy (random selection) is killed unless SECURITY and MEDICAL present.

EVENT — STAR TREK THE NEXT GENERATION

PARTICLE SCATTERING FIELD

A Tamarian Ship used a particle scattering field to charge the atmosphere of El-Adrel IV, stranding Jean-Luc Picard and Dathon on the planet in 2368.

Plays on one of your ships with a Particle Scattering Device. No beaming to or from a planet is allowed where ship present. You may discard Field at any time.

INTERRUPT — STAR TREK THE NEXT GENERATION

EYES IN THE DARK

Deanna Troi saved the U.S.S. Enterprise in 2369 by communicating through nightmarish visions with a telepathic species on the other side of a Tykan's Rift.

Plays when facing a dilemma. If Empathy present, add the skills and attribute numbers of one personnel (random selection) from your opponent's ship (your choice).

D'Tan — STAR TREK THE NEXT GENERATION

CIVILIAN

Romulan boy. A bright and active member of Spock's underground. Once showed Spock Romulan artifact depicting the syllabic nucleus of the Vulcan alphabet.

☑ Youth   ☑ Archaeology
☑ Where present, Romulans without Treachery are INTEGRITY +1.

| INTEGRITY | 7 | CUNNING | 6 | STRENGTH | 3 |

INTERRUPT — STAR TREK THE NEXT GENERATION

KEVIN UXBRIDGE: CONVERGENCE

A Douwd, a race of sentient energy beings of "disguises and false surroundings." He is capable of using his enormous powers to stop threats with a single thought.

Destroys all Event cards in play at any one spaceline location (including those on ships).

INTERRUPT — STAR TREK THE NEXT GENERATION

KEVIN UXBRIDGE: CONVERGENCE

A Douwd, a race of sentient energy beings of "disguises and false surroundings." He is capable of using his enormous powers to stop threats with a single thought.

Destroys all Event cards in play at any one spaceline location (including those on ships).

Brute Force

Vult Minor: Suppress Krieson rebels seeking foothold here.

STRENGTH=10 x number of Away Team members present (minimum 3 personnel)

INTERRUPT — STAR TREK THE NEXT GENERATION

COUNTERMANDA

A Federation student enters when she discovered her true identity as a Q. Amanda took a dim view of the over-manipulative use of power upon other species.

Nullifies Telepathic Alien Kidnappers OR if opponent just played Res-Q or Palor Toff, suspend that action, look through opponent's discard pile and put any three cards out-of-play.

INTERRUPT — STAR TREK THE NEXT GENERATION

DEVIDIAN FORAGERS

Disguised beings from Devidia II traveled to troubled times and spopuld places to steal and consume neural energy from souls who would not be missed.

Look through any one discard pile and place two personnel out-of-play. Add their attribute numbers to one of your icon personnel for this turn.

DILEMMA — STAR TREK THE NEXT GENERATION

PUNISHMENT ZONE

On Rubican III, mediators arrested Wesley Crusher when he fell into a garden. He was designated for death, which created a Prime Directive dilemma for Jean-Luc Picard.

One Away Team member (random selection) is killed OR beam up that personnel at a penalty. Double penalty if Federation.   -5

Qualor II Rendezvous

Qualor II: Rendezvous with nefarious merchants in squalid camp.

Treachery + Greed OR Amarie
Aligned personnel on planet in stasis until mission can...

INTERRUPT — STAR TREK THE NEXT GENERATION

HAIL

Using a universal translator and other communication technology, such as at Worf's station aboard the U.S.S. Enterprise, starships can greet any ships they encounter.

Plays on any ship "flying by" one of your ships; it must stop at your location. OR Select two ships; they cannot battle each other this turn.

EVENT — STAR TREK THE NEXT GENERATION

THE MASK OF KORGANO

In legend, Masaka was chased by Korgano across the sky like the Iceman moon chases the sun. Jean-Luc Picard masked himself as Korgano to fool Masaka.

Plays on one of your personnel. While in play, changes it from normal to ▣ icon personnel, or vice versa.

EVENT — STAR TREK THE NEXT GENERATION

RISHON UXBRIDGE

In his grief, the Douwd Kevin Uxbridge re-created his dead wife, Rishon. As if she were real, he responded to her stubborn tendency to keep him calm at tense moments.

Plays atop one Event card in play. Protects the underlying event from Kevin Uxbridge. However, Kevin Uxbridge may remove (discard) Rishon. (Not cumulative.)

❷

1. Star Trek CCG Expansion Set

Alternate Universe
pack of 15 cards
Decipher Inc., USA, 1995
$4

2. Star Trek Customizable Card Game

Starter Pack, 60 White Border cards
Decipher Inc., USA, 1994
$12

3. ST TNG Customizable Card Game Player's Guide

Decipher Inc., USA, 1996
$18

The Star Trek Customizable Card Game (or ST CCG) is a card game
in which the player is supposed to carry out individual missions against
a partner. The more cards the individual player possesses, the more
likely he is to be able to carry out a mission successfully. Some cards
support each other, others block each other or take away
collaborator's, strength or energy points. In any case, this game is a
science in itself.

❸

Trading Cards

2. ST: CCG Warp Pack

Decipher Inc., USA, 1995
This pack of cards was given away free. The cards were supposed to help CCG beginners who did not have many cards. They also allow the White Border player to cleverly circumvent another player's strong cards. In this combination they were available only in this set, even though individual cards could also occur in an Expansion Pack.

1. Individual Cards for ST: CCG

Various "rare" black-and-white border cards
Decipher Inc., USA
Prices vary according to demand

3. Star Trek: The Card Game (Classic)

Starter Pack, 60 cards
Modern Graphics, D 1996 $12

4. ST: The Card Game (Classic)

Booster Pack of 15 cards
Modern Graphics, 1996
$3

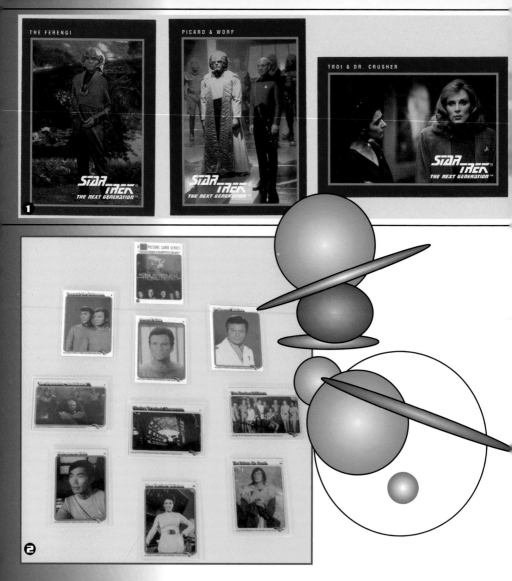

1. Star Trek 25th Anniversary Trading Cards

printed on cardboard
Impel Marketing Inc, USA, 1991
individual packs:
$2.50
complete set:
$38

2. St: The Motion Picture Trading Card Set

printed on cardboard
Topps, USA, 1979
$30

3. SkyBox Master Series

six-card packs
SkyBox, USA, 1994
individual pack of 4:
$30
complete set
$38

SkyBox
MASTER SERIES

CHECKLIST A

1. St: TNG
"The Episode Collection"

Season Two, 8-card packs
SkyBox, USA, 1995
individual packs:
$2.50
complete set (108 cards):
$25

COMMANDER WILLIAM T. RIKER

❶

❷

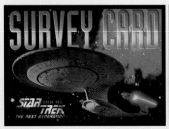

2. St: TNG
"The Episode Collection"

Season Three, 8-card packs
SkyBox, USA, 1995
Individual packs:
$2.50
complete set (108 cards):
$25

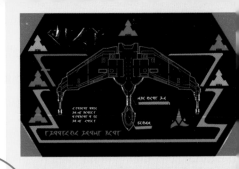

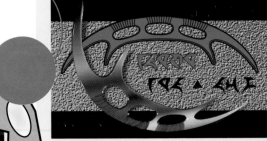

**1. Klingon Special Cards,
Season One Star Trek: TNG
The Episode Collection**

**2. Klingon Special Cards,
Season Two Star Trek: TNG
The Episode Collection**

3. Klingon Special Cards, Season Three Star Trek: TNG The Episode Collection

SkyBox, USA
These Klingon cards are special cards from the individual episoded
A set of three costs $38

4. Foil-embossed "K'Ehleyr" Card

Special card from the 5th season of ST: TNG The Episode Collection
SkyBox, USA
$12

KLINGON™ VESSELS OF THE 23rd CENTURY

U.S.S. GRISSOM™ NCC-638
OBERTH CLASS STARSHIP

FERENGI MARAUDER™

ORION PIRATE SHIP

U.S.S. RELIANT™ NCC-1864
MIRANDA CLASS STARSHIP

U.S.S. SARATOGA™ NCC-1867
MIRANDA CLASS STARSHIP

S.S. HURON NCC-1913
FREIGHTER CLASS VESSEL

VULCAN SHUTTLE™

U.S.S. EXCELSIOR™ NCC-2000

①

1. Star Trek: Reflections of the Future

Phase One
SkyBox, USA, 1996
Individual pack
$3
complete set (100 cards) $30

2. Special Cards: Undercover Major Kira Cardassian Star Trek: Reflections of the Future

Phase Two
SkyBox, USA
Individual card: $18
set of all 9 cards: $155

3. Special Chrome Card: Star Trek: Reflections of the Future

Phase One
SkyBox, USA, 1996
Individual card: $18
set of all 9 cards: $155

4. Skymotion Card: Enterprise 1701-A

thick plastic card with 25 holograms that show a brief "film" when card is moved
Star Trek: Reflections of the Future
Phase One
SkyBox, USA $88

5. Ship's Register Gold-Plate Trading Card ST: Reflections of the Future

Phase One
SkyBox, USA, 1996
Individual card: $55
set of all 9 cards: $500

The price of this card series is so high because the likelihood of finding one in a pack is only 1 in 72.

UNDERCOVER

Major Kira™

2

MID-23RD CENTURY
Communicator™

3

A-TREK™

4

U.S.S. STARGAZER

5

TOSK

JEM'HADAR

VIDIIAN

MORN

CHANGELING

BANEAN

TRILL

HUNTER OF TOSK

KAZON

①

UNSTABLE WORMHOLE

SOUL OF SKORR

MURASAKI 312

'RAKOSAN FIGHTERS

NAGILUM VOID

OUTSTANDING MAKEUP
"Cost of Living"

②

❸

OSMIC STRING FRAGMENT

1. Star Trek: Reflections of the Future

Phase Two
SkyBox, USA, 1996
Pack of cards:
$3
complete set (100 cards):
$30

2-3. Star Trek: Reflections of the Future

Phase Three
pack of 8 cards
SkyBox, USA, 1996
Per set:
$3
complete set (100 cards):
$30

❶

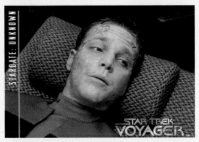

1. ST: Voyager Season Two

pack of 8 cards
SkyBox, USA, 1996
$3 per pack
complete set: $30

2. "Holodoc" Trading Card

with original Robert Picardo autograph
SkyBox, USA
$90

Trading Cards

1. Star Trek Generations

Widescreen Cards
SkyBox, USA, 1994
$3 per pack
complete set:
$30

2. Star Trek First Contact

Widescreen Cards
SkyBox, USA, 1996
Per pack:
$3
complete set (60 cards):
$25

❶

STAR TREK: FIRST CONTACT™ CHECKLIST

Common Cards:
1. A Dedicated Vessel
2. The Nightmare
3. The Neutral Zone
4. U.S.S. DEFIANT™ Off-Line
5. BORG™ Sphere
6. Unto the Breach
7. Zetrom and Lily
8. BORG™ Meteor
9. Historic Date
10. 21st Century Civilians
11. Lily Opens Fire
12. Lily Faints
13. The Phoenix
14. Heating Up
15. Sickbay Goes Dead
16. "Please State the Nature..."
17. Drinking With Zetrom
18. The Hive
19. Firefight
20. Lt. Commander Data™ Captured
21. Assimilated

22. Captain Jean-Luc Picard™ and Lily
23. BORG™ Drones
24. Talk of the Future
25. View From the Stars
26. BORG™ Queen
27. Real Skin
28. Borgified Starship!
29. The Return of Dixon Hill
30. Nightclub Entrance
31. A Ruby Kiss
32. BORG™ in the Night
33. Missile Complex
34. Barclay Meets a Legend
35. Reports of My Assimilation
36. Lily Meets Lt. Commander Worf
37. Lost in the Woods
38. Suiting up for Zero G
39. Lieutenant Commander Data™ the Rebel
40. Pain and Pleasure

41. Interplexing Spires
42. Hull Fight
43. Deflector Separation
44. True Motives
45. Objection Noted
46. Lost Friend
47. Phoenix Launches
48. Databorg
49. Captain Jean-Luc Picard™ Faces the Queen
50. The Return of Locutus™
51. Sacrifice
52. Target Phoenix
53. Phoenix Hits Warp
54. Hive Collapse
55. Close Encounter
56. First Contact!
57. Back on Duty
58. New Friends
59. U.S.S. ENTERPRISE™ Crew
60. Checklist

3. Special First Contact Deanna Troi Card

Character Card stamped, high-gloss
individual cards:
$10
set of ten:
$25

1. Picture on Linen

art print
Kelly Frears, USA, 1976
$18

2. TNG Nameplate

hand-embroidered banner
40 hours' work
One piece made by Giuseppe Puliga,
Ludwigshafen
material worth $10
actual value not calculable

3

3. Mount Selaya
wool carpet, hand-knotted, six-months' work
one piece by Karina Büthgen, Wittenberg
material worth $625

1. U.S.S. Enterprise Crew Identification

2. Quark's Bar Gold Card

A real alternative for travelers with little luggage. Whoever is worthy of Ferengi credit must know something of business . . .

3. Space Station Visa

For all DS9 visitors who
do not belong to the Federation.

All three cards by
Antioch Publishing Co., USA, 1994
$2 each

4. ST: Federation Passport

Passport for Federation members with advice and warnings for strange worlds.
Pocket Books,
USA, 1996 $8

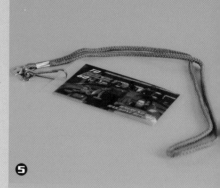

5. Backstage Pass, Paramount Studios

with cord
Starflight Enterprises, USA $15

This makes the owner look important, but nothing more. In spite of this "pass," one gets only to the entrance of the studio and not inside where it is really interesting — on the closed-production sets.

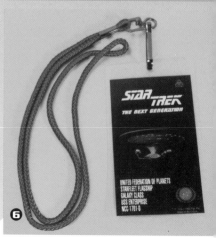

6. Enterprise Visitor's Pass

with cord
Icons, USA, 1992
$15

7. Pseudo-Starfleet Passes

Medical Units
Starlight Enterprises, USA
$6 each

8. Pseudo-Starfleet Passes

various areas
Starlight Enterprises, USA
$6 each

9. Official Bridge Pass

card allows entrance to the bridge
Antioch Publishing Co., USA, 1992
$6

10. Official Crew Identifiaction Card

crew member ID
Antioch Publishing Co., USA, 1992
$6

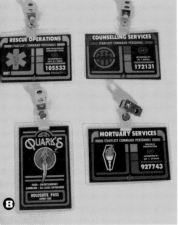

SAMMELSURIUM

1. Star Trek Original Film Cels *Relics*
limited edition of 475 pieces, with certificate
Paramount Pictures Corporation, USA, 1994
$125-plus

3. Star Trek Hologram
Klingon warship
A.H. Prismatics, Britain
$30

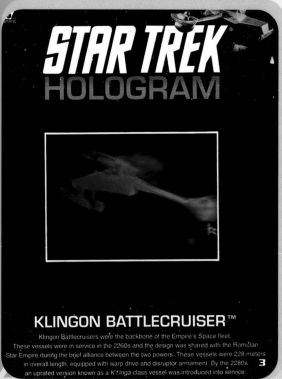

2. Star Trek Original Film Cels

The City on the Edge of Forever
limited edition of 650 pieces, with
certificate
Paramount Pictures Corporation
USA, 1994
$125-plus

4. Star Trek DS9 Hologram

the station in orbit
limited edition of 50,000 pieces
with certificate
A. H. Prismatics, Britain
$30

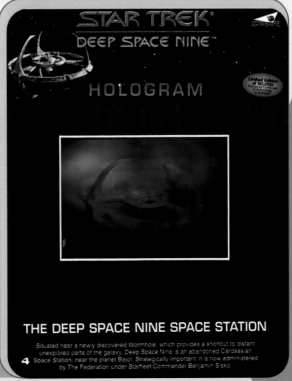

THE DEEP SPACE NINE SPACE STATION

Situated near a newly discovered Wormhole, which provides a shortcut to distant
unexplored parts of the galaxy, Deep Space Nine is an abandoned Cardassian
Space Station, near the planet Bajor. Strategically important, it is now administered
by The Federation under Starfleet Commander Benjamin Sisko.

SAMMELSURIUM

1. Mini-Tricorder
Captain's Patent & Phaser
(with holder)

Burger King, USA, 1993
given out with Kids Club orders
as part of a Star Trek promotion
value not known

2. Laser Spex
prism glasses

A. H. Prismatics Ltd., Britain
$6

An absolute must for freaky dreams in the space
disco.

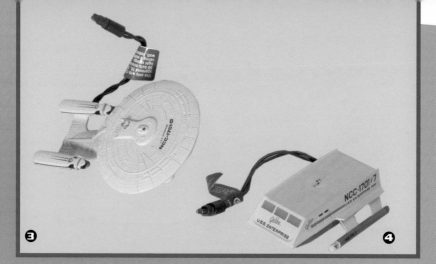

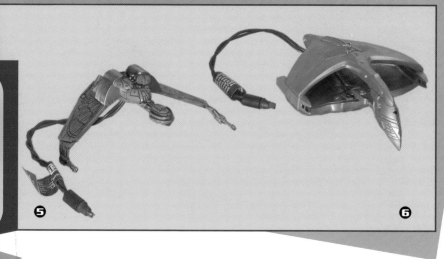

Christmas Ornaments

3. U.S.S. Enterprise 1701 D
with lit engines
Hallmark, Canada, 1993
limited, no longer made
$95

4. Shuttle Galileo
with acoustic Christmas greetings
from Mr. Spock
Hallmark, Canada, 1992
limited, no longer made
$310

5. Klingon Bird of Prey
with lit bridge and engines
Hallmark
Canada, 1994
limited, no longer made
$95

6. Romulan Warbird
with lit engines
Hallmark
Canada, 1995
limited, no longer made
$95

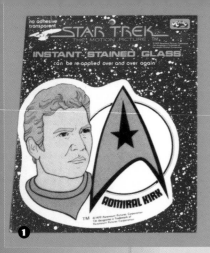

1. Admiral Kirk Window Foil

attaches to glass without adhesive
P.P.C., USA, 1979
$3 each

2. Mr. Spock Window Foil

attaches to glass without adhesive
P.P.C., USA, 1979
$3 each

Star Trek:
The Card Game

German version
Skybox- Modern Graphics,1996
$1.25 each

4. U.S.S. Enterprise
1701 Decal

P.P.C., USA
$1.25 each

5. Capt. Kirk &
Mr. Spock Decal

P.P.C., USA
$1.25 each

6. "Hailing Frequencies Open"
Sticker

Creation Convention, USA
$3 each

CARDASSIAN MILITARY SCHOOL

BAJORAN FREEDOM FIGHTERS

STARFLEET ACADEMY
SAN FRANCISCO, EARTH • "Ex Astris, Scientia"

❼

ROMULAN MILITARY ACADEMY

KLINGON WARRIOR ACADEMY

❽

BORG INSTITUTE OF TECHNOLOGY

FERENGI SCHOOL OF BUSINESS

7. Windshield Stickers
can be applied to rear window
of car from inside
various designs and letterings
P.P.C., USA
$6 each

8. Windshield Stickers
can be applied to rear window
of car from inside
various designs and letterings
P.P.C., USA
$6 each

SAMMELSURIUM

1. Cup with Cardassian Face
limited edition
Applause, USA, 1994
$25

2. Cup with Q in Judge's Robe
limited edition
Applause, USA, 1994
$25

3. Cup with Geordie LaForge
limited edition
with certificate
Applause, USA, 1994
$25

4. Cup with Neelix Face
limited edition
with certificate
Applause, USA, 1994
$25

5. "United Federation of Planets" Ceramic Cup
metallic motif
Rawcliffe, USA, 1994
$20

6. "U.S.S. Enterprise" Ceramic Cup
metallic motif
Rawcliffe, USA, 1994
$20

7. Ceramic Cup with Ferengi Emblem
metallic motif
Rawcliffe, USA, 1994
$20

8. Ceramic Cup with Gold Lettering
various designs
P.P.C., USA
$25

9. "Classic Command Symbol" Ceramic Cup
metallic motif
Rawcliffe, USA, 1994
$20

10. "Classic Science Symbol" Ceramic Cup
metallic motif
Rawcliffe, USA, 1994
$20

11 Warp Cup
with no-skid base, it doesn't spill, even at fastest acceleration in a swinging space ship!
$30

12. Exclusive Convention Coffee Cup
limited — only for guests and workers
P.P.C., USA
$30

⑤ ⑥ ⑦

⑧

⑨ ⑩

THIS VEHICLE TRAVELS AT
WARP SPEED
STAR TREK

⑪

CREATION ENTERTAINMENT
proudly presents
William Leonard
SHATNER NIMOY
THE 25-YEAR MISSION
tour
© 1992 CREATION ENTERTAINMENT

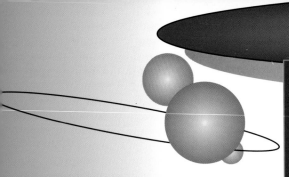

1. Ceramic Beer Stein with Classic Enterprise on Metal Lid

limited edition of 1966 pieces, with certificate
DramTree-CUI, USA, 1996
$155

2. Star Trek Glasses

(stamper, whiskey glass, Beer mug)
heavy smoked glass with gold printing and rim
P.P.C., USA, 1994
$20 for stamper
$30 for whiskey glass and Beer mug

Guinan's secret for special occasions: Useful in any
home bar, not only in 10 Forward!

❶

❷

3. Plastic Drinking Cups

various motifs
P.P.C., USA
$10 each

4. Thermos Cup

insulated insert
keeps drinks cold
P.P.C., USA, 1994
$28

For all those times when it gets hot in the engine room!

SAMMELSURIUM

1. "Star Trek—The Crew" Porcelain Plate

28-day limited production
Enesco Corp., USA, 1993
sold for $65 each

2. "Mr. Spock" Porcelain Plate

25th Anniversary Edition

3. "Capt. James T. Kirk" Porcelain Plate

25th Anniversary Edition
14-day limited production
The Hamilton Collection, USA, 1991
sold then for
$65

4. "Dr. Leonard McCoy" Porcelain Plate

25th Anniversary Edition

5. "Montgomery Scott" Porcelain Plate

25th Anniversary Edition
signed by James Doohan
The Hamilton Collection, USA, 1991
sold then for
$65

6. "William T. Riker" Porcelain Plate

7. "Capt. Jean-Luc Picard" Porcelain Plate

14-day limited production
The Hamilton Collection, USA, 1993
sold then for
$65

8. "Captain Kirk" Porcelain Trading Card

14-day limited production
The Hamilton Collection, USA, 1993
sold then for $65

9. "Captain's Own" Porcelain Set

set consists of plate, saucer, and cup
limited, signed by William Shatner
Pfalzgraf, USA
value not known

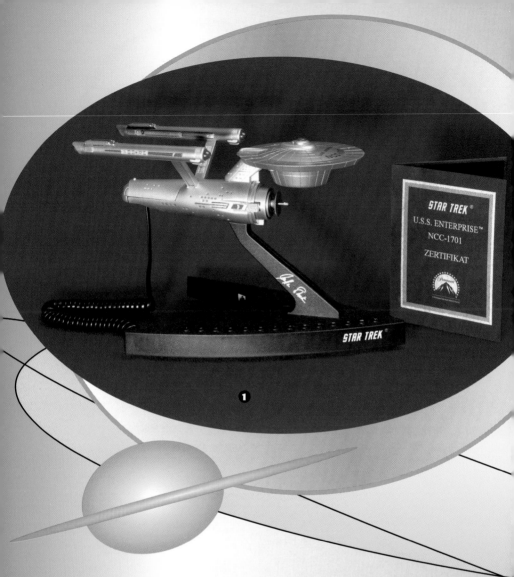

1. Star Trek Telephone

limited edition
with certificate
mailable
Herweck GmbH, Germany, 1993
$140

2. United Federation of Planets Flag

limited edition of 1,000 pieces, with certificate
Flaggen Pohl, Mittenwald, Germany
$30

3. Deep Space 9 Door Hanger

"I've been sent to . . ."
Antioch Publishing Co., USA, 1993
$3

4. Voyager Door Hanger

"Unexplored Territory"
Antioch Publishing Co., USA, 1995
$3

2 UNITED FEDERATION OF PLANETS

DOORKNOB HANGER
Use on any door, or any place!

I've been sent to
Space Station
DEEP SPACE
NINE!

STAR TREK
DEEP SPACE NINE

3

STAR TREK
VOYAGER

DOORKNOB HANGER
Use on any door, or any place!

WARNING
ENTERING
UNEXPLORED
TERRITORY

4

BEAM ME UP SCOTTY! THERE'S NO INTELLIGENT LIFE DOWN HERE.

TRANS WARP DRIVE

❶

1. Refrigerator Magnet

Drawing by James Doohan, autographed cannot be bought, as Doohan gives this object only to people he likes.

2. Fan drawing

Autographed
by James Doohan, 1981
Single piece
valuation not possible

3. Original drawing by George Takei Autographed

drawn in Hamm City Hotel, 1996
valuation not possible

4. Saber

with George Takei's autograph
material vlaue $110
single piece, valuation not possible

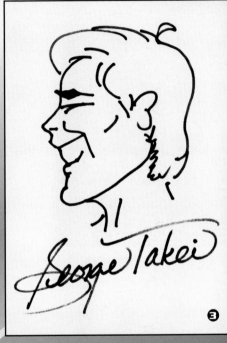

SAMMELSURIUM

1. "Riker" with Autograph

mounted on plate
first series, limited to 2,500 pieces
P.P.C., USA
$150

2. "Picard" with Autograph

mounted on plate
first series, limited to 950 pieces
P.P.C., USA
$172

3. Program Excerpt with Photo of Marina Sirtis

April 1985

4. Autograph of Marina Sirtis

April 1985

5. Production Photo Marina and Colleagues

Photo by Chris Augustin, 1985

6. Group Picture: Rocky Horror Ensemble, Deutsches Theater, Munich, 1985

Crew member Marina Sirtis, top row, third from right
Photo by Jürgen Garbade

(A few clippings from the pre-Star Trek days. About half a year later, Marina Sirtis, on a tourist visa, went looking for a job in Hollywood. The rest is history.)
At this point, hearty thanks once again for a really wonderful time, to all who were there!

MARINA SIRTIS
"Magenta", "Columbia"

Ausgebildet an der Guildhall School of Music and Drama. Ihre Repertoir-Arbeit schließt die Ophelia in "Hamlet" ein, die Argentinierin in "Falkland Sound", die Linda in "Stags and Hens", die Rirette in Sartres "Intimität" und erst kürzlich spielte sie die Esmeralda in "Der Glöckner von Notre Dame". Im Fernsehen war sie zu sehen in den Serienproduktionen "Raffles", "Hazell" and "Minder" und "Who Pays The Ferryman?" Weiter in "The Kelley Monteith Show", "Speak for Yourself", "Everybody Here" und "Muck and Brass". Filmrollen spielte Marina in "The Thief of Baghdad", in einer Neuinszenierung von "The Wicked Lady" mit Faye Dunaway und Alan Bates, in "Blind Date", sowie in "Space Riders" mit Barry Sheene. ❸

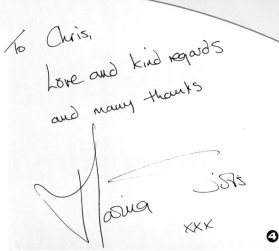

To Chris,
Love and kind regards
and many thanks

Marina Sirtis

xxx ❹

5

6

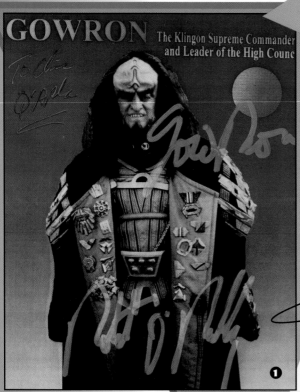

GOWRON The Klingon Supreme Commander
and Leader of the High Counc

**1. Autograph of
Robert O'Reilly**

Hamm, Germany, 1996

**2. Autograph of Andrew
Robinson**

"The Brave Little Tailor,"
Hamm, 1996

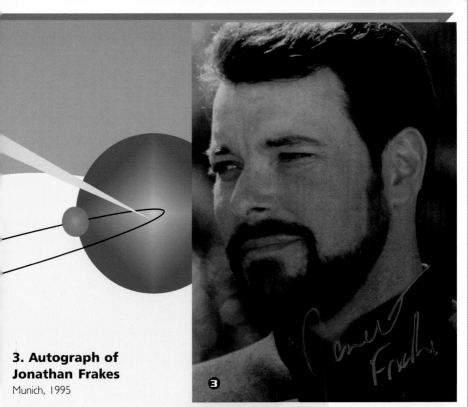

3. Autograph of Jonathan Frakes
Munich, 1995

4. Autograph of Dwight Schultz
Hamm, 1996

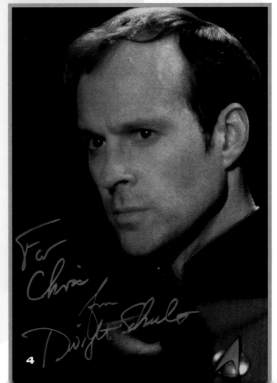

SAMMELSURIUM

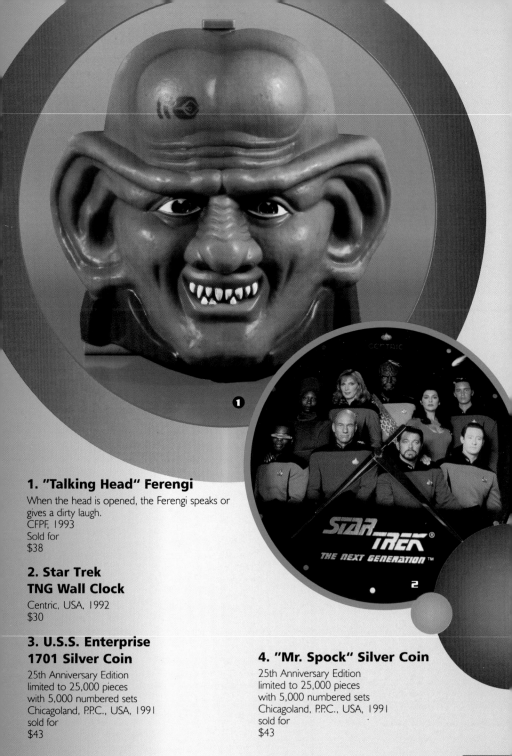

1. "Talking Head" Ferengi

When the head is opened, the Ferengi speaks or gives a dirty laugh.
CFPF, 1993
Sold for
$38

2. Star Trek
TNG Wall Clock

Centric, USA, 1992
$30

3. U.S.S. Enterprise
1701 Silver Coin

25th Anniversary Edition
limited to 25,000 pieces
with 5,000 numbered sets
Chicagoland, P.P.C., USA, 1991
sold for
$43

4. "Mr. Spock" Silver Coin

25th Anniversary Edition
limited to 25,000 pieces
with 5,000 numbered sets
Chicagoland, P.P.C., USA, 1991
sold for
$43

5. "Captain Kirk" Silver Coin

25th Anniversary Edition
limited to 25,000 pieces
with 5,000 numbered sets
Chicagoland, P.P.C., USA, 1991
Sold for
$43

SAMMELSURIUM

1. "A Klingon Challenge" Interactive Board Game

German Edition,
no longer made
MB-Spiele, Germany, 1993
$55

2. Three-dimensional Chess Game

Plexiglas, blue-and-gold chessboards,
silver and gold figures
Franklin Mint, USA/Germany, 1990
limited edition
$310

3. Three-dimensional Chess Game

Single piece
handmade, 200 work hours
Made of cast iron, marble tiles, and painted terracotta stones as
playing pieces
Material value $220
Present value not calculable

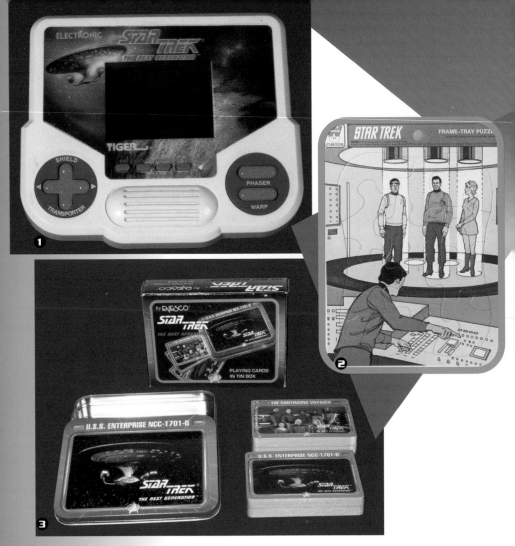

1. ST: TNG Electronic Game

Tiger Electronics Inc., USA, 1988
$10

2. Star Trek Frame-Tray Puzzle

Western Publishing Company Inc., USA, 1979
Original price approximately 50 cents
present value not known

3. Star Trek TNG Playing Cards in Zinc Gift Box

Enesco, USA, 1992
Value not known

4. Introduction to Roleplaying: How to Host a Mystery

In the package are a diagram of the U.S.S. Enterprise D, invitation cards, directions, "hidden hints," an audio cassette, and the leader's instructions. The game begins with a written invitation to six players. They meet at a predetermined place that offers plenty of room for action (a weekend in a hotel or youth hostel would be ideal). There the players get an overview of what has happened and their instructions, in which the most important facts in the case are explained and the "role" of each player is described. After that, each player behaves as his role description specifies until the end of the game. Information is to be gathered and clues are to be found. Naturally, one tries to find out who has done what with whom, and why. In short: "Clue" live!
Decipher Inc., USA, 1992

Forum

Fandom can only exist when you have people who are, as they are generally called, "fans." "Fans" is a designation that I don't actually like because it generalizes a group of people who are quite different into one "mass." For the uninitiated, there are all types of fans, from the "crazed fanatic" to the "detail-loving modelmaker" to the "silent admirer." The boundaries between the individuals are not at all clear, but flow into each other.

To the many Star Trek fans whom I have met as a "free collaborator" at conventions in the course of the last five years, I must really express great praise. They are almost all extremely disciplined and polite. They behave properly in a hotel, and often wait for hours in long lines for autographs without pushing, until they can finally be near their favorite for a couple of minutes.

At this time, two large conventions with up to 3,500 visitors, and about ten smaller ones with 50 to 500 visitors, take place in Germany every year. The events are held in a range of sites, from simple halls in youth guest houses, with one star guest, to the ballrooms of luxury hotels with five or more star guests. Every convention, whatever the size, is always a terrific experience for all who take part because there is so much to see and experience. And often, really entertaining things happen, both in front of and behind the curtains. It is a difficult task for a coordinator to organize such a convention, since they must please both the "fan" and the host.

The promoter, who spends a lot of money to make the convention possible, and bears a huge responsibility for the guest stars, visitors, and helpers, is one side. He has a right to expect that his staff of helpers will do everything to guarantee a smooth run for the convention and, in the event of an accident or glitch, the coordinator must avoid mass panic and make the very best if things and somehow "keep the show running."

On the other side is the "fan," or rather the convention visitor, who in the short space of a weekend wants to experience as much as possible. Often they have saved for months for this visit in order to be able to afford a hotel room, the trip, and the admission fee.

Between the two parties there naturally, and very quickly, develops a conflict of interests if everything doesn't go off smoothly, whether it be a technical problem because the technician forgot to change the frequency for the video projector so that the program is shown in the wrong hall, or the radio contact between the various control posts produces incomprehensible transmissions that have to be circumvented somehow, thus resulting in delayed entry to the autograph party. Or perhaps there is a problem with the "star guest." Maybe he or she was scheduled for 9:30 a.m., but the escort and chauffeur got hung up in the morning traffic jam, or the guest overslept. This calls for a lot of patience and coordinating capability from all participants.

But enough of that; on the following pages a forum is provided for people who take part in fandom actively and spend a lot of their free time, energy, and, most importantly, their money in order to live their very personal part of the Star Trek dream. All the pictures and text in the Forum were made available to us by the participants themselves. The individual statements do not necessarily represent the views of the author and publisher!

I have called this chapter "Forum" very deliberately, because this assortment of individuals is not at all "representative." On the contrary, most of the people are friends of mine. I turned to them first because, in the short time between the planning and the publishing of this book, there was simply not enough time to send out a "call" for fans.

Whoever is interested in seeing himself on these pages in the future is welcome to get in touch with the publisher and we'll organize everything from there!

Marc alias Lt. Kendra Varani in custom-tailored DS9 uniform coveralls

Since about 1978, Marc has been "Enterprise-infected" and he has been an active fan for some five years. His coveralls are made of the best woolen cloth and have a full-length zipper. The cost of such a custom-tailored uniform, depending on the tailor and the price of the cloth, is around $250. As a good model builder, he has made several nice pieces that decorate his apartment. He has become known for a device made to "tune" the TNG Tricorder, which, alas, is no longer produced. With an expenditure of some $75 for the materials (the price of the tricorder plus electric components like wires, running lights, light diodes, etc.) and some three months of work, a tricorder can be rebuilt so that it can scarcely be told from the series-produced original.

Marc also produces data recorders PADD's himself, though it must be noted that he does not do this for commercial reasons. A data recorder made by Marc can only be obtained as a gift (naturally with reimbursement for the cost of the materials) and each one is a unique, individual object! To make it one needs a piece of wood 3 millimeters thick, a coping saw, wood putty, suitable laminated pictures, glue, and some eight hours of patience.

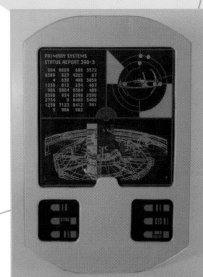

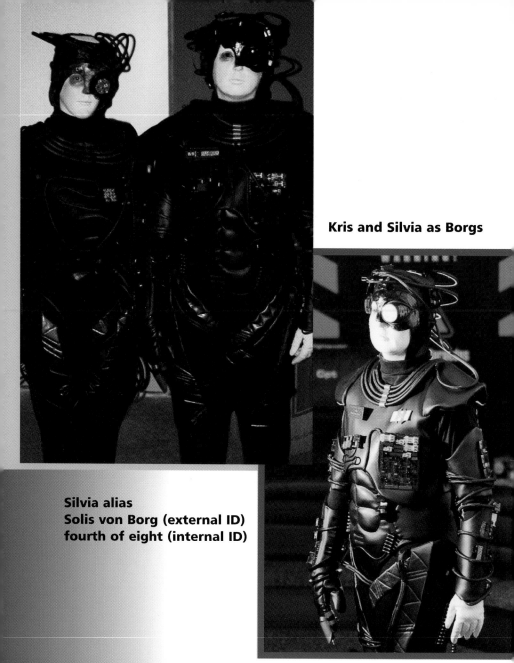

Kris and Silvia as Borgs

**Silvia alias
Solis von Borg (external ID)
fourth of eight (internal ID)**

Personal note:

I became a Star Trek fan at about the age of six and loved to create whole space fleets out of Lego blocks. My fleet, though, had only one type of ship. All the ships looked like the "Enterprise," as far as that was possible with Legos. And now I make Borg costumes. They are worn (rumors to the contrary notwithstanding) only at conventions and photo sessions!

And why Borg?

Once upon a time there was . . . no, seriously. It began at a convention in Munich in 1995. I had already visited a convention previously, but what I got to see in Munich exceeded all my expectations. There were crowds of people in homemade costumes. The perfection with which those costumes were made was simply amazing. And I stood there in my green jumpsuit. Of course, I had picked it out and bought it myself, but only bought it. When I looked at the great costumes, I got the idea of trying my hand at costume creation and going to the next convention in my own outfit. But what kind of an outfit, that was the question? It ought to be something that was not seen very often. Thus neither a Vulcan nor a Klingon. All sorts of ideas ran through my head — Ferengis, Cardassians, Romulans, or the hunters from the DS9 story, *Tosk, the Hunted*? But the costume always struck me as being too warm. While I racked my brains, I looked at the people who got photographed again and again. Well, I had never been one of those people who like to be photographed before. Friendly smiles and all that. Somehow, all the photos in which I was supposed to smile looked frightful. Good — so it was clear that it had to be a character that did not smile. And it should also have a calm temperament, not like the Klingons. At first the Vulcans popped into my head again, but they were already represented in goodly numbers. "BORG" came to my mind, and why not? It would be difficult, but also uncommon. And I had never yet seen a Borg smile. In the series, they usually just stood around uninvolved until they were activated. I could do that too, thus the decision was made. Of course I had no idea . . .

Costs and Materials:

There are a great many possibilities for building a Borg. Here is what went into one of my costumes:

• 3 x 1.50 m black imitation leather	$65
• 3 x 1.50 m black cloth	$12
• 40 m of 6 mm plastic isolation tubing	$30
• 40 m of 8 mm joint-sealing tubing	$30
• 10 meters of step-muffling material, (enough for about three costumes)	$55
• Motorcycle gloves (imitation leather)	$30
• White cloth gloves	$12
• Welding goggles	$12
• Glass for the goggles (ground to fit)	$65
• Various wire cables	$12
• Copper foil	$6
• Laser pointers	$40-125
• Fasteners (as decoration)	$12
• Spray paint	10 to $12
• Diving mask (if you don't want to sew the hood)	$30
• 1 meter roll of tape	$6
• 1 meter of 10 millimeter elastic band	$5
• Motocross boots	$190
• Liquid latex	$17
• Make-up (theatrical quality!)	$30-65

  (3 gray tones, 1 white, 1 black, fixing powder or
  spray, cold cream, tissues, wipes, make-up brush)
- 1 belt
- black turtleneck sweater, black leggings
- plastic toys (robots, airplanes, etc.)
- Computer junk
- Any quantity of Superglue

Unknown participant in a costume competition

Note the material used in this Cardassian's homemade two-piece armor: papier-maché, thick cords, glue, and paint.

And why a Cardassian?

To the superficial observer, Cardassians often appear to be hostile, sneaky, coldhearted, agressive, brutal and racist reptiles. But evil also has its fascinating side, and often inhabits the most interesting personalities. These eternal "good-guy" Starfleet types with their peace-and-joy diplomacy! As a pseudo-Cardie, one can really bring out the dark corners of one's soul, as one neither can nor will in real life. But on closer observation, one realizes that Cardies are one of the most multi-level races that the Star Trek universe has ever produced. The Vulcans are always just logical, Federation types are often bureaucratic bores (the exceptions prove the rule!), Klingons usually behave like kids just into puberty, Romulans seem chilly and distanced, Ferengi are arch-capitalists with a fear of women, Borg nothing more than machines without a will of their own, and our Bajoran friends usually represent a naive, bucolic race of religious fanatics. Cardassians are cool, calculating, arrogant, and rational. Yet a remarkable depth of feeling slumbers in them. They treasure the coziness of a harmonious family life, and their women are very emancipated. Cardies enjoy pleasure, guzzle Kanar or Red Leaf tea, pamper themselves with delicacies of all kinds, like cozy warmth, and admire stylish architecture and elegant clothing. For me, they are simply a race with mental strength and the right mixture of hardness and decadence.

**Cornelia alias
Legate Tharania Dukat**

This armor consists of:

- Basic form of styrofoam
- covered with shaped acrylic latex
- the added "bones" are made of aquarium tubing
- the dots in the central area were cast in liquid latex with the help of a car mat
- sleeves and side panels of the armor are made of stuffed bouclee cloth

Cost of the materials $155, plus about three months of work

One can also put original outfits together
using ready made parts
as demonstrated by
Marcello as a Ferengi,
who decorated a ready made rubber mask,
a suitable suit from a flea market,
and an impressive necklace.
Now the enterprising businessman
of the future is ready.

**A few impressions from a
Star Trek convention:**

**A Vulcan
family in
traditional costume**

**A young Romulan
in a homemade
uniform**

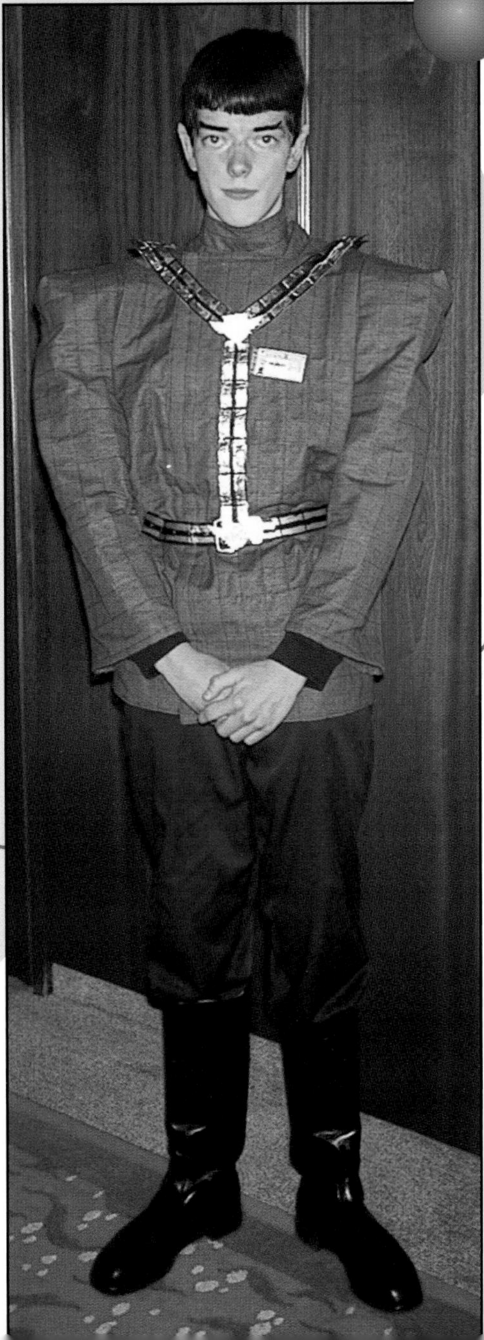

Klingon Daggers in various styles:

left: Warbird Bowie
center: Warbird Dagger
right: Raptor Knife
all daggers are made of stainless steel, lavishly decorated,
and produced by Gil Hibben, USA
Prices begin about $125, depending on what country one buys them in

"*etih QorghHa'lu'chugh ragh 'etlh nIqvu' 'ej jejHa'choH*"
"Even the best blade will rust and become dull if it is not taken care of"
— old Klingon saying

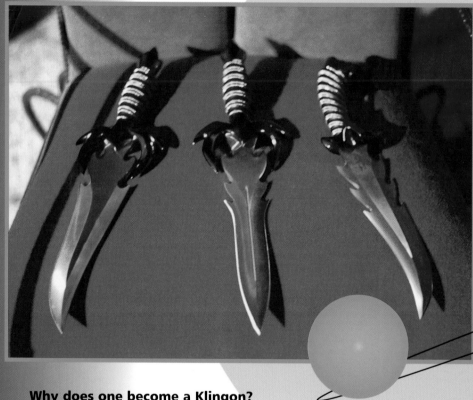

Why does one become a Klingon?

- Wearers of Federation uniforms are too "soft" or "languid"
- ... and too "uniform" or "replaceable"
- Change into a dangerous, honorable Klingon warrior
- Live out the "other" side of our existence
- Individual uniform/outfit
- Be a strong character with an appropriate mask
- Klingon weapons do not have such a dehumanizing effect
- Lots of fun and good feeling
- And nobody will recognize you without the mask!

Falk in a Klingon warrior's outfit

Personal data:

Falk has been a Klingon for about a year and a half and has made everything himself, from the mask to the costumes. Even a Bat'telh (half-round swordlike weapon) is part of his equipment.

The mantle consists of heavy coat material and leather, the armor of metal and leather.
Cost $250 plus one to two months' work.

Pictures from a Klingon Meeting

Whoever would like to make contact with the Klingons and has internet access may contact:
http:\\www.khemorex-klinzhai.de

Thomas
in full uniform
as a Vulcan

Homemade
red TNG uniform
made by Thomas

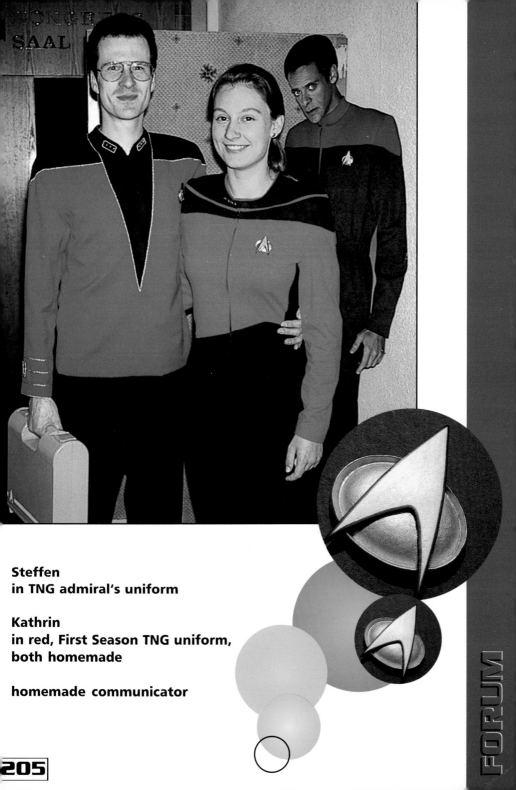

Steffen
in TNG admiral's uniform

Kathrin
in red, First Season TNG uniform,
both homemade

homemade communicator

FORUM

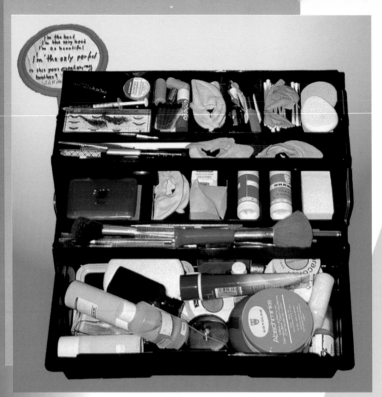

A look into Thomas's make-up kit

At a Trek dinner, Thomas told me the following story about
the origin of his Vulcan ears and the beginning of the Data family
beloved by Star Trek fans:

"...for the next convention (Munich in 1995) I made myself the red TNG uniform and
appropriate trousers. In addition, Katrin, Steffen, and I planned to take part in the
costume competition at the convention as the "family." So we set out to sew the
costumes. Steffen made himself the yellow uniform of Data and built an android
headpiece out of batteries, wires, and light diodes. Katrin sewed Lai's dress with
Steffen's help. My job was making Lore's coveralls. The false ears I bought were not
perfect enough for my Vulcan outfit, so I got busy and made myself some. Steffen
helped me to cast my "genuine" ears. My ears were covered with a cardboard rim, and
the hairs with plastic wrap. Finally a mixture of casting powder and water was made
while I waited, lying on my side on the floor, Steffen slowly poured the material over
my ear. After fifteen minutes the mixture had hardened, and Steffen carefully took the
negative form off me. This form was then cast in Keramin (a plasticlike material). When
this had hardened, I had a positive cast of my ear. With modeling material I created the
Vulcan ear points, which was not at all easy. Using liquid latex, available in the make-up
trade, these ear models were brushed seven or eight times. Every layer had to dry for
at least an hour before the next layer could be brushed on. To make them stay on, I
used Mastix, a special hair adhesive for beards and latex parts, available as stage make-
up. The transitions between skin and latex ears were covered with a thin film of liquid
latex. When my face and ears were covered with the same make-up, you could no
longer tell that the ears were false."

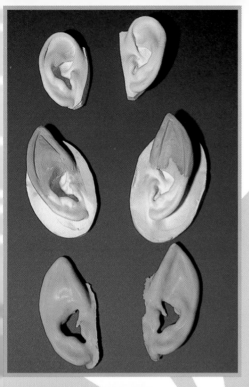

The three stages of ear production:
normal casting
modeled ear points
finished latex ears

Close-up of the shaped ear points

Close-up of the finished latex ear.

A typical photo of the "Data Family"
from the left, Thomas as "Lore,"
Katrin as "Lai,"
and Steffen as "Data."

Spacecraft Highlander

No other role-playing group in the world of Star Trek fandom is more loved and hated than the crew of the U.S.S. Highlander, under the command of Robert Amper, alias Captain Norad. At this point we can say at once that the Highlanders are not half as bad as their reputation. And in this forum, some of the prevailing prejudices and half-truths shall be done away with at last and the Highlanders shall be seen as what they really are: a devoted group of friends who enjoy science-fiction and role-playing adventures and yet stand firmly with both feet on the ground of reality in private life.

The crew of the U.S.S. Highlander is a group of people who take pleasure in live role-playing. Their stage, though, is not a board with scenery and figures on the living-room table, but the "bridge of a spaceship."

And whoever thinks it is a space with colorful posters and a few pieces of cardboard scenery is very mistaken. To make the bridge, a living room measuring about 25 square meters was rebuilt, a project involving more than a year's work. In the rear of the room is a lit-up, raised area with three leather seats and two stand-up controls for security and weapons systems, completely disguised doors, a "main screen," which is supplied with animations and films via video projection, and not least, the four lit-up control panels for additional bridge personnel.

All in all, this is an impressive scene. An architect, two specialist builders, a team of four electricians, and two carpenters worked to transform Robert Amper's designs into a real, usable spaceship-bridge scene. One, in fact, that was not just built for a video and then torn down again, but a solid, built-in, fully functioning setup! The cost of all this was considerable; the contracted work alone cost about $50,000. We won't even talk about the cost of materials.

Every year there are four big Highlander meetings, in which up to 25 crew members, who live all over Germany, meet in Munich. And they meet in full uniforms and masks! A meeting lasts from Friday evening to Sunday afternoon and takes place according to clear rules. One of the leaders of the game, whose name is kept secret, is to carry out a mission created in a week of preliminary work. And all sorts of things can happen. Once the crew met at 2:30 a.m., in a dripping-wet, pitch-black forest, to rescue the captain and command team from the grip of evil aliens.

Then as now, though, the high point of the meetings is the "Away Mission," in which the crew "operates" outside under real action conditions, with campfire, grill, and torches, but also night sentry duty, discussion of action, and a tour of a cave as the main attractions. Despite all the fantasy (which also plays a major role here), the first rule is: Safety first! There are equipment lists that are checked for completeness. Beginning with head and knee protectors, through spare batteries, to the indispensible chemical emergency light. There is no place here for self-styled heroes. Anyone who gets out of line at such an event can endanger the whole group. And the danger is real, not play-acted. For that reason, discipline is also demanded.

The most important prerequisite for membership in the Highlanders is a goodly share of imagination. Every member creates an independent character (who must not exist in film or on television!) and works up a fictitious life history for his invented character. And, as much as we hate to say it, since membership in the Highlanders is a very desired position, there are no vacant positions at this time. Only when the two hundred people on the waiting list are taken care of can new applications be considered again.

From left to right:

Lt. (JG) Mirtek, Science; Lt. (JG) T'Para, Assistance Counselor;
Captain Norad; Lt. (JG) Trivia, Mission OPS; Cmd. Lavender, Main
Counselor; and Lt. Mc Fly, Chief Science.

Robert Amper alias Captain Norad

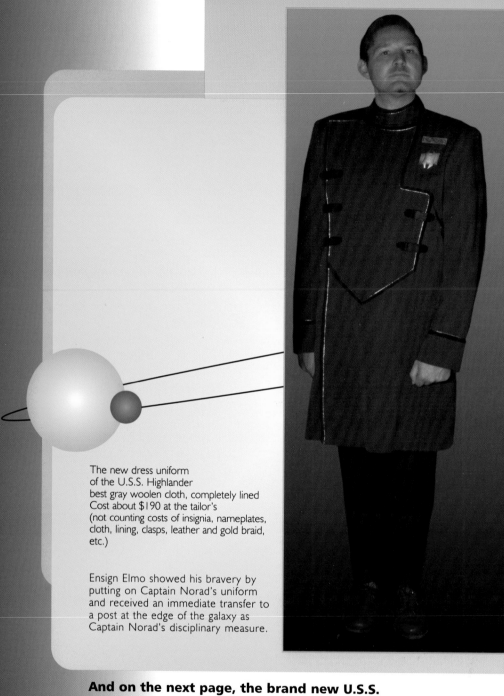

The new dress uniform
of the U.S.S. Highlander
best gray woolen cloth, completely lined
Cost about $190 at the tailor's
(not counting costs of insignia, nameplates,
cloth, lining, clasps, leather and gold braid,
etc.)

Ensign Elmo showed his bravery by
putting on Captain Norad's uniform
and received an immediate transfer to
a post at the edge of the galaxy as
Captain Norad's disciplinary measure.

And on the next page, the brand new U.S.S.

Created by computer magician Tobias Richter after a design by Robert Amper,

The Highlander emblem and
the angular insignia of rank
Specially made for the role-playing group.
They can now be bought for $18
Rank insignia $4

The normal "work clothes"
of the U.S.S. Highlander's crew
The stripe shows what type of work the
wearer does. Blue is for medicine and
science, yellow for technology and security,
all members of the command level —
captain, navigation, and weapons control —
wear red.

Here, too, the best black wool gabardine is
used, and the uniform is lined. The costs
are between $95-125 (here too, the costs
of the nameplate, emblems, insignia of rank,
cloth, lining, etc., are extra).

Highlander, NCC 2404-A makes its first great appearance.

who is also responsible for the design drawings of uniforms and insignia.

FORUM

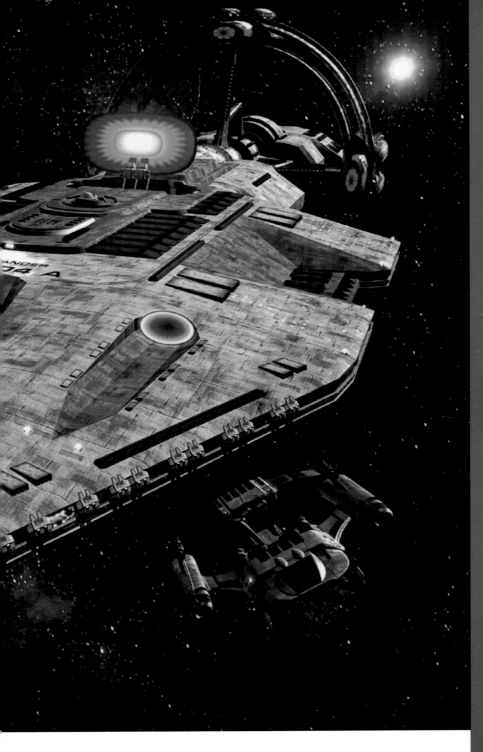

Admission ticket, program, pin, and bag from *Star Trek: The Exhibition*

From October 26, 1996 to January 26, 1997, at the Josef-Haubrich-Kunsthalle in Cologne, there was:

Star Trek: The Exhibition.

It was the only site of the exhibition in Germany. The price of admission was pleasantly low, and thus the promoters were very pleasantly surprised by the great number of visitors, not only Star Trek fans.
The reactions of the visitors ranged from great praise to negative criticism because the exhibition had been on view in London a few months before and had presumably been somewhat more inclusive than in Germany.

But no matter which way the criticism went, it was still an interesting look behind the scenes of a series cult that had lasted more than three decades. Many of the displays — "knowing" visitors said — have now vanished from the set through natural "erosion" and/or were "cobbled up" out of lowest-cost materials to save money.

In films, just as in the theater, all that matters is the effect of a piece of scenery or a costume under studio lights, nothing else! And if a cheap item looks fantastic under the stage lights, why should it then be made better and more expensive? Besides, most of the pieces (especially hand-held items like "phasers," etc.) are junked anyway after the film is finished, either because they are no longer wanted or because new designs have replaced the old items. In this business, nothing is meant to last forever (even if the fans see it differently!).

In spite of all that, the exhibit offered an interesting look into the creative work of a film production company. For model-building freaks and people who make their own costumes and masks, there was lots of inspiration there. Rarely have I seen so many people with sketch pads or cameras at an exhibition!

For all those who could not travel to Cologne, the following pages contain a few excerpts from the exhibit.

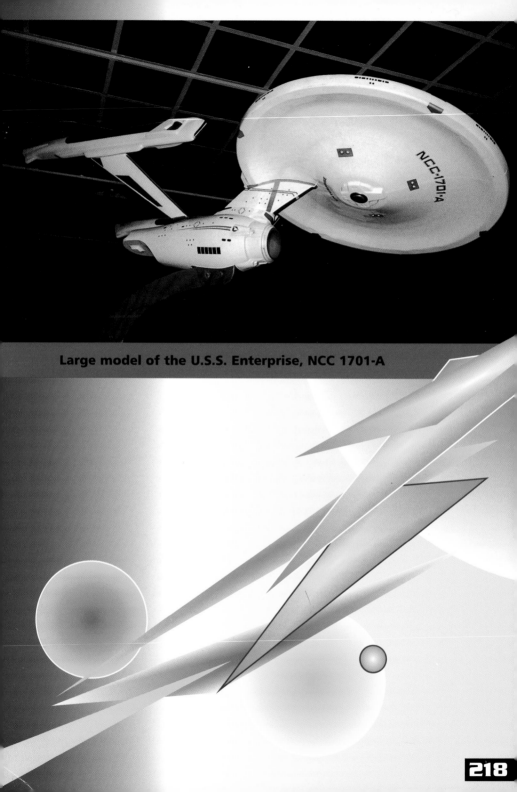

Large model of the U.S.S. Enterprise, NCC 1701-A

Life-size model of the classic bridge

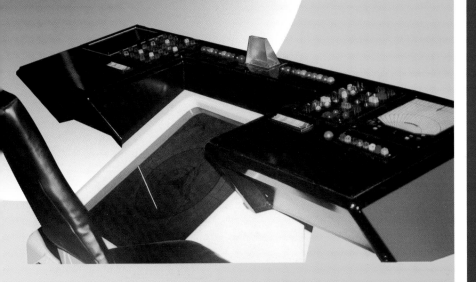

Close-up view of the navigation panel

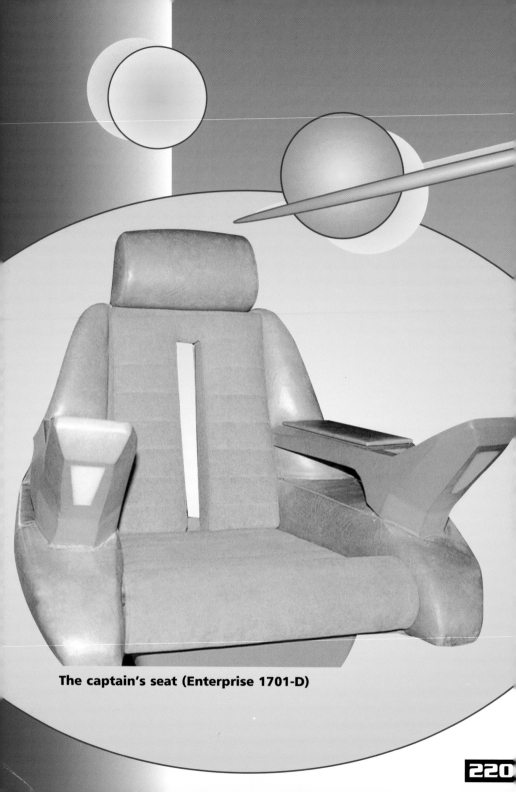

The captain's seat (Enterprise 1701-D)

The Captain's readiness room (Enterprise 1701-D)

Jean-Luc Picard's uniform

A large set piece from
Star Trek — The Next Generation

Something for model builders — a destroyed building made of unconventional individual pieces . . .
children's toys, plastic junk, drinking cups, etc., 30 by 20 centimeters

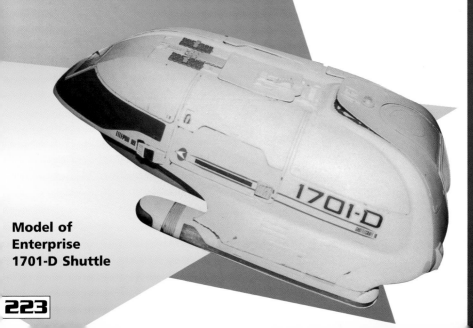

Model of
Enterprise
1701-D Shuttle

upper left
Khan's Costume from the second Star Trek movie, "The Wrath of Khan"

upper right
Mr. Spock's Vulcan robe from the third and fourth movies: *In Search of Mr. Spock* and *Back to the Present*

lower left
General Chang's Warrior Robe from the sixth movie: *The Undiscovered Country*

Chief Engineer Montgomery Scott's Uniform from the second to seventh movies

14-year-old Technical Lieutenant's protective coveralls, from the second to sixth movies

A Klingon Uniform from the Classic Series

"reH boch qutluch lo'lu'bogh"
or **"The used honor dagger always gleams!"**
— old Klingon saying

**Armor of the
Klingon Warrior**

**A Mask of a
Klingon Warrior**

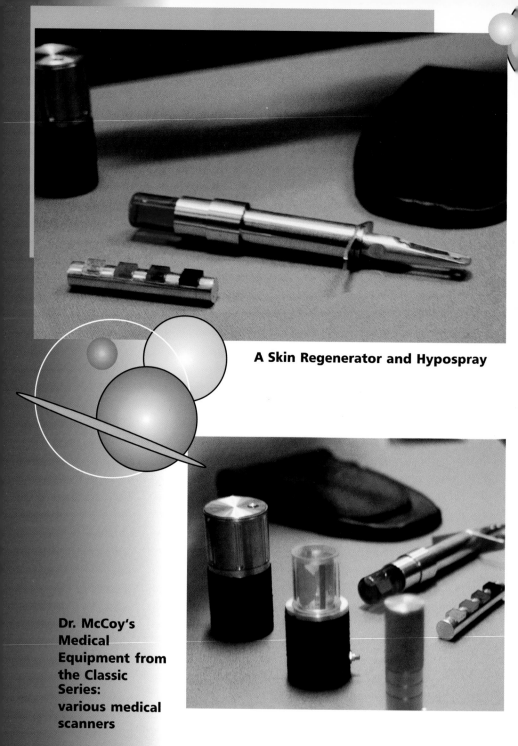

A Skin Regenerator and Hypospray

Dr. McCoy's Medical Equipment from the Classic Series: various medical scanners

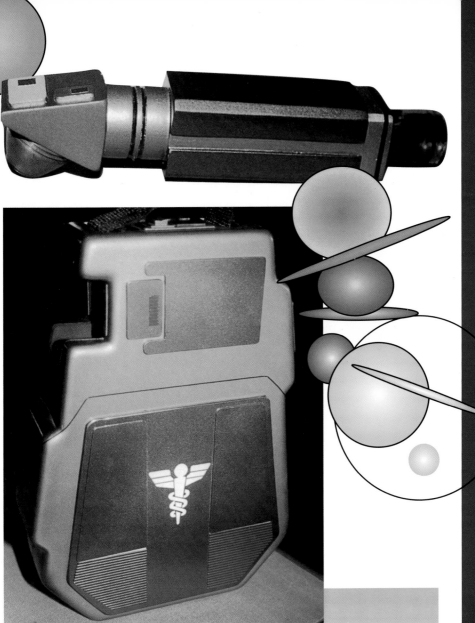

upper picture
**The devices were developed further:
Dr. Crusher's Hypospray from *The Next Generation***

lower picture
**Everything is at hand in case of emergency:
The Doctor's Bag from *The Next Generation***

A Ferengi Mask

A Ferengi Uniform

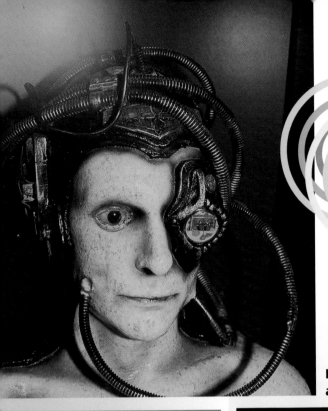

**Details of
a Borg Mask**

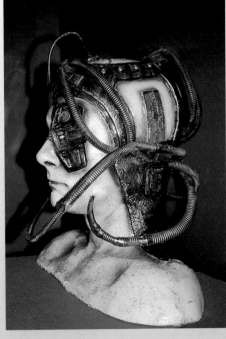

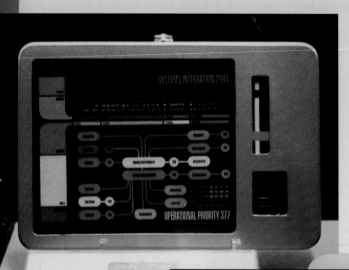

SYSTEMS INTEGRATION 2984

OPERATIONAL PRIORITY 377

Technical PADD with Structural Chart

Bajoran PADD (Personal Access Data Display)

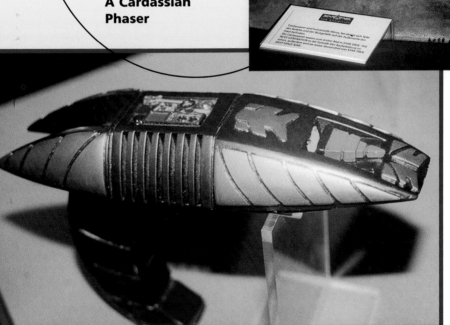

A Cardassian Mask

A Cardassian Phaser

Jem'Haddar Warrior

Tosk, the Hunted

Morn, the silent steady guest at Quark's

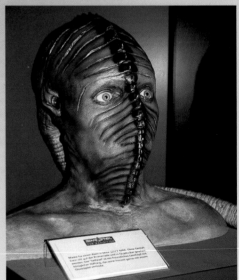

An unidentified guest at Quark's Bar

And with this blaster, Dr. Tholian Soran sent Captain James T. Kirk into the Hereafter in the seventh movie, _Generations_. Various _Next Generation_ Communicators

1. From the other timeline of "All good things"
2. Used in all movies since _Generations_ (DS9 & VOY)
3. From the episode _Future Imperfect_ (with integrated insignia of rank for Commander)
4. The communicator of the "next generation," used through _Generations_